W9-BRW-438

BARE BLASS

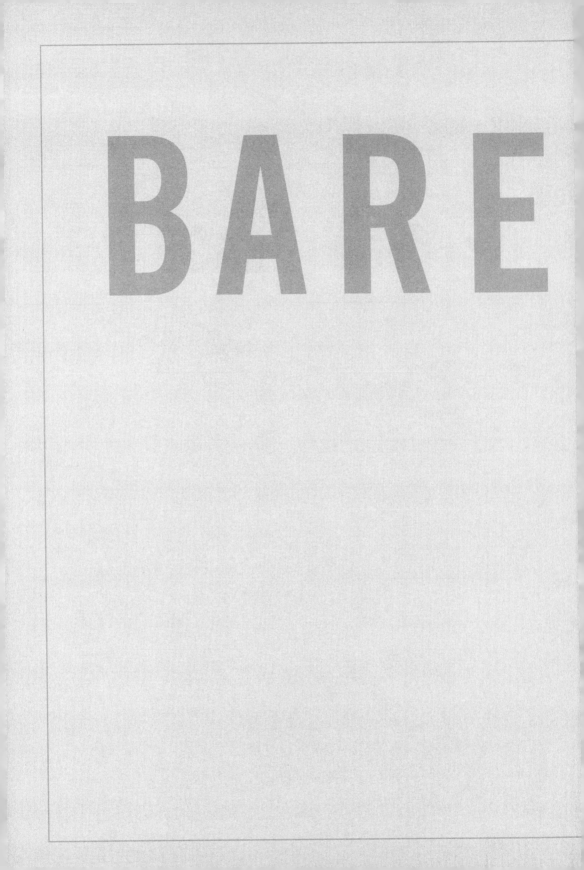

BARE

BLASS

BILL BLASS
EDITED BY CATHY HORYN

HarperCollins*Publishers*

BARE BLASS. Copyright © 2002 by the Estate of Bill Blass. All rights reserved. Printed in the United States of America. No part of this book may be used or re-produced in any manner whatsoever without written permission except in the case of brief quotations embodied in critical articles and reviews. For informa-tion, address HarperCollins Publishers Inc., 10 East 53rd Street, New York, NY 10022.

HarperCollins books may be purchased for educational, business, or sales promotional use. For information, please write: Special Markets Department, HarperCollins Publishers Inc., 10 East 53rd Street, New York, NY 10022.

An extension of this copyright page appears on pages 183–184.

FIRST EDITION

Designed by Joel Avirom

Printed on acid-free paper

Library of Congress Cataloging-in-Publication Data
Blass, Bill.
    Bare Blass / Bill Blass ; edited by Cathy Horyn.—1st ed.
        p. cm.
    Includes index.
    ISBN 0-06-018555-4
        1. Blass, Bill. 2. Fashion designers—United States—Biography.
    3. Costume design—United States—History—20th century I. Horyn, Cathy.
    II. Title.

    TT505.B537 A3 2002   2002068482
    746.9'2'092—dc21
[B]

02 03 04 05 06 ❖/RRD 10 9 8 7 6 5 4 3 2 1

Life's great, life's grand,
Future—all planned.

—Cole Porter, from the song "Ridin' High"

CONT

ENTS

BARE BLASS

1

Then and Now

Childhood bores the hell out of me.

I think it bored me even as a child, although I am certainly aware that had it not been for the joylessness, colorlessness, and fatherlessness of my small-town Indiana childhood, I might not have gone anywhere. People today speak about the character-building qualities of the miserable childhood, but I can tell you from experience: There is nothing like the dull, unattractive childhood to give a bedazzled boy the *right* push.

Of course, the beauty of my upbringing was in its plainness. And there was this consoling feature: Everyone we knew in Fort Wayne, and everyone they knew, were in the same plain boat. As a consequence of having little money ourselves and no social standing above my mother's widowed respectability—and even here we might have stood to gain some ground if my father had died instantly and unambiguously in a highway crash rather than by a self-inflicted gunshot in our front parlor—I learned, perhaps in that single isolating moment (I was five), how to occupy myself. In this stiff-upper-lip wholesomeness there was surely somewhere a budding genius for avoiding anything unpleasant or ugly (what else am I to make of a drawing I did at the age of six showing a butler serving drinks in a Manhattan penthouse, other than, perhaps, an advanced knowledge of where the better customers lodged?). But at that time, in a life-in-

general way, I was happy. And don't forget the world was a different place then. It didn't take much to amuse a kid, and everybody had troubles, on account of the Depression, so there was no point complaining about that. I used to spend hours up in my room, flopped on my bed, reading the latest *Vogue* or *Delineator* and marveling at the unapproachable glamour of "Lady in Emerald Hat, coiffure of ostrich." Fashion held such mystery then. On Saturdays, I and my friends would go down to the local movie house, with its aromas of sweat and cigarettes and drugstore perfume, and watch in gaudy silence as Marlene Dietrich breezed through sixteen costume changes in *The Garden of Allah*. Even food had wondrous possibilities. I remember once being at the cottage we had on a lake, about sixty miles from Fort Wayne, and after a quick evaluation of our supplies, settling on sandwiches made of cold leftover mashed potatoes, with lavish swirls of Miracle Whip (this was before we knew about Hellmann's) and lots of black pepper on the soft white bread. You can't imagine how delicious those sandwiches tasted. There would be other meals as wonderful and bad, like the spur-of-the-moment dishes we made in the army during the Second World War when a fresh egg was available. But I think that day at the lake was the first time I realized that the taste of food depends not just on the ingredients, but also on where you are at the time, and how hungry you are.

I was lucky in one respect. My type of looks, which were the opposite of the type that appealed to me, were wholesomely innocuous to fit into several local categories, sissy to jock, while belonging to none. This may strike you as a bit of very un-American foot-dragging toward the inevitable main event—sex, and sex with *whom?*—and given the expectation today that every memoir writer will conduct himself with the thoroughness of a House Committee on Un-American Activities investigation, telling all, I suppose I am ducking (for the moment) the question of sexual category, though, even then, I didn't believe in them. Sexual encounters between men were far more prevalent among my classmates at Southside High School than encounters with women, in part because so few of the girls were willing to do it with their boyfriends, and because homosexuality, being so forbidden, was so tempting to accomplish. I recall a Sunday-school teacher gathering a group of us boys around for what we assumed would be another grim lesson about the Apostles and him saying rather jovially, "Let's do something different for a change. You guys know what a circle jerk is?" Some of us did and some of us didn't. Needless to say, none of us saw a religious tie-in. But I doubt that the teacher, or the kindly men posing as father figures or even the more sweetly observant boys that I knew, most of them destined for marriage, considered themselves homosexuals.

As for myself, I was much more interested in joining worlds that before the war would have been denied to a middle-class boy with only a high school education, and this meant, at the very least, getting out of Fort Wayne. Luckily, as I say, my looks, along with a sense of humor, helped me to straddle the different divides, and by the time I was nineteen, I had added, for good measure, the polish of a slight British accent—no doubt lifted from Frederick Austerlitz, a.k.a. Fred Astaire, another Midwesterner. Yet, curiously, it wasn't until I was in the army, living for the first time among men, that I experienced real happiness. And freedom.

Also, I could draw. The beauty of being able to draw, or paint, from an early age is that you never feel trapped, least of all by your immediate circumstances. When I was fifteen, I began selling sketches of evening dresses, at $25 a pop, to a manufacturer in New York called Kalmour (long gone) that did a brisk business selling to women who plainly saw themselves, as I saw Dietrich and Swanson, entering a room and insolently flinging their wraps down on the couch.

I didn't make much off the Kalmour people, but it was enough to help pay for fashion school in New York. A few years later, in Europe during the war, I managed to fill several of the small notebooks that we all carried—all of us being creative types assigned to a rather enigmatic outfit called the 603rd Camouflage Battalion—with miniature drawings of ladies hats, shoes, gloves, and dresses. I still have those notebooks. The man closest to me in the army, Bob Tompkins, who today lives in Gardnerville, Nevada, recently told me that I drew my first sketch of my company logo, a pair of mirrored B's, while lying on a bunk in a convent in Luxembourg as we were waiting to go up to the Battle of the Bulge. I have no memory of this. He also reminds me that from the day we first met in boot camp, at Fort Meade, Maryland, until the night we came home from the war, on July 5, 1945, and took the elevator up to the apartment in Greenwich Village where my mother and sister had moved from Indiana (and where Bob's wife, Bunny, now waited, too), I seemed to be smiling for dear life, and, according to the photographs I have, he is right.

In retrospect, I can see how certain influences of my childhood and youth entered my unconsciousness and remained there, like a fine fog, while I steered unaware, and apparently grinning, toward the only city I have ever wanted to live in (New York) to do the only thing I have ever wanted to do (fashion). For all my ardent interest in movies, I must have recognized that Hollywood was no place for a relatively insecure lad still lean and scared from the Depression; it all looked *too* easy and glamorous, and that made me nervous. I needed the beat and grind of New York, the feeling of being hemmed in, the discomforts, and the macaroni and cheese you could only get at the Automat. Inevitably, my clothes displayed a similar taste for realism—admittedly, a jazzy, expensive realism—that occasionally put me on the outs with fashion editors, especially Diana Vreeland, who in the sixties kept *Vogue* filled with the Turkish delight numbers that appealed to her love of fantasy, but which generally were unavailable in stores. I minded the rejection—up to a point. Some years ago, at a meeting with other Seventh Avenue designers to discuss a show, it became clear to me that they were only interested in showing novel or outrageous clothes, and not the kind their customers actually bought. Finally, someone said, "We don't want those kind of people." To which I replied from my place at the back of the room, "I'll take 'em."

I did get to know a lot of actors after the war, but then one did in those footloose days. New York had an exalted air of newness and excitement about it; you felt that anything was possible. Cary Grant became a friend. So did Kim Stanley, who would sometimes model for me between plays; and, a little later, Jerry Robbins, Josh and Nedda Logan, and Irene Selznick, who was Louis B. Mayer's daughter and supposedly a pain in the ass, but we always got on well. I met her through Slim Keith, with whom I was also quite friendly—for a while. But apart from dressing actresses and listening to their stories, which were fascinating, Hollywood was never part of my plans. I remember being in Acapulco one January after

the collections. In those days—I am speaking now of the fifties, before anyone outside a small world of debutantes and editors took an interest in designers—the practical thing for a Seventh Avenue manufacturer was to send his designer off on a long holiday after each collection. That way the bosses, who were imaginative only about making a buck, could change the clothes and make them more salable. So I got to see a lot of the world in its first postwar bloom. Spain. Morocco. Cuba. I went to Cuba a lot. Cuba was great fun; sex, too.

But Acapulco: I was there on one of those long vacations, in 1958, and every day on the beach I saw Lana Turner and her hustler lover Johnny Stompanato. You can imagine how conspicuous they were. She may have been common, but she was blessed with the best figure—and that hair. Even the police dog she had attending her on the beach had white hair. Anyway, we got to talking, and she said, "Do you want to come over for dinner?" I told her I had plans, but the truth was, I wasn't interested in Lana Turner. Stompanato, of course, was unbelievable—though it hardly matters what he was; he'd be dead in a few months. Maybe if she had been Dietrich or someone of that caliber, I might have mustered the proper interest.

No, I can see how the plainness of my upbringing influenced me. It affected my eye, for one thing, though not immediately. I was intrigued a few months ago when John Richardson, in the course of contributing his memories to this book, mentioned that he had visited my first grown-up New York apartment, at 444 East 57th Street, during a brief period in the seventies when I had loaned it to a mutual friend, Bat Stewart, Lady Batista Stewart, a wonderfully funny English dame, who preceded my friendship with John by nearly a decade. Perhaps inevitably, too, that apartment, which I had bought from Suzy Parker in 1959 when I finally had enough money put together, was a penthouse with a wraparound terrace and a butler named Hugh. Working for the first time with Chessy Rayner and Mica Ertegun of the decorating firm MAC II, I had the walls of my bedroom covered in a tortoiseshell fabric, then lacquered to a high shine. There were low banquettes in the living room, with a few modern paintings, collections of objects, and a pair of soaring impala horns on one of the tables. I thought the place perfectly reflected who I was at that time, and in a way it did.

Here is what John said:

Joe Eula's sketch of Niki de Gunzburg and me at the Ritz Bar.

Everything was kind of brown and beige and chic, and Billy Baldwinish. Nothing wrong with it, impeccably done, but it could have been anyone else's apartment. It was a chic man's apartment, with a slight emphasis on the masculinity—which is a terrible mistake.

He's absolutely dead-on right. In all that excessively polished masculinity, I was harboring doubts about myself. Slowly, though, over the past two and a half decades, I've stripped away most of those transparent affects, saving the odd piece, until I got down to a more austere backdrop that emphasizes (and reveals) precious little. Bare wood floors. Plain white walls hung with a few good drawings. A minimum of objects, but all with a maximal sense of scale and drama. Chessy, who shared my distaste for eye-jarring lamps or anything so practical as conversational groupings of furniture, once said that she thought the reason I had so few comfortable chairs in my Connecticut house (and these invariably occupied by one or more of my dogs), was that I didn't like having too many people around. Quite true: up and out! And, if anything, my eye has grown more severe in its judgments. Sometimes I have a desire to burn everything, or at least walk out and go someplace else and start over. Be seventeen again.

Which, of course, is the past coming back to me.

But I have rarely talked about my childhood, certainly not in so many words, and usually with a peripheral interest, as though I were circling an earlier self I no longer recognized. I've never felt the slightest need to share the secrets of my youth or love affairs—another un-American activity. Nor have my friends been inclined to fault me in this. They already think they know everything anyway. "Oh, Bill, we know all about your life." End of subject. (Curiously, when word got around that I was doing a book, they struck a different note: "Oh, Bill will never talk about his personal life." A gauntlet? Or worry over what I might say about them? Hah!) When I was working on Seventh Avenue and journalists would ask me about my early years, naturally I'd repeat the same goddamn lines "Yes, my father committed suicide when I was five . . . a terrible loss . . . always knew I'd leave Indiana . . . just a question of when . . . " This became infinitely easier with the arrival of computerized databases, which would just regurgitate everything I had said, though occasionally errors were introduced into the cud— among them that I had played high school football and, more unbelievable, that I had once been married. A fiction composed by a lady publicist eager to beard me—and a rather hoary one, considering that I've never lived with another human being since returning home from the war. Dogs, yes.

I am aware, of course, of certain patterns that formed in my childhood: on the minus side, a lack of affection, or display of affection, that surely accounts for my inability to relate to others on an intimate level; a need for keeping up appearances that was part of my mother's refusal to discuss my father's death, and which is why I avoid any kind of conflict or emotional entanglement. And there is this odd association: For as much as I have adored women—dressed them, placated them, jollied them out of whatever misguided hope they had—the moment one of them gets it into her head to take *possession*, I am sliding toward the door. No one can get his coat on faster. It's always the same reaction: panic followed by . . . "Got to go!"

When I left Fort Wayne in the summer of 1940, ineluctably joining a conga line of Hoosiers escaping for New York or Hollywood (ahead of me was Norman Norell, behind me would be Halston, and somewhere up the line were Cole Porter and Carole Lombard), I was seventeen. I was tall, blond, and lath thin. Except for a trip the previous summer to the World's Fair and another to Chicago to visit our one rich relative, a great-uncle who lived in high style at the Edgewater Beach Hotel and whom my mother had hoped I would impress (evidently I didn't since we never heard from the man again), all my knowledge of the world was confined to a single Midwestern city of 118,000 inhabitants. My first home in New York was the YMCA. And here in this Christian hostelry, where so many American families sent their sons to live cheaply before marriage, it was a revelation to me that, in addition to bedbugs, same-sex flourished as single-mindedly as it had in Fort Wayne. So, in one respect, I wasn't innocent. Eventually I moved into an apartment in the West 60s with a group of guys—junior ad executives, bankers-in-training, each of us with his own box of cereal and carton of milk in the icebox—and I went to work as a sketch artist for a sportswear house called David Crystal, making $30 a week. Nowadays, young designers, if they are any good, receive million-dollar contracts, first-class air travel, and chauffeured cars; in the forties and even after those of us came home from the war and were still in uniform, we weren't permitted to ride in the same elevator with our employers. We were backroom boys in the grubby business to end all grubby businesses—Seventh Avenue. By the sixties, that would all change, and we, some of us, would become part of one of the most audacious boy's clubs ever conceived—and largely because of one man, John Fairchild, publisher of *Women's Wear Daily*, who pitted designer against designer, socialite against socialite, and in that constantly shifting breach, helped to create a new, more modern business—American fashion.

But if it's true, as Bob Tompkins said, that I drew my first sketch of my corporate logo in 1944 while lying on a bunk in Luxembourg, then it would be another fifteen years before I would have a product to put it on, and another ten after that before I had my own name on the door. Patience is something I know a lot about.

When I set out in the spring of 2000 to write my memoir, I wasn't big on nostalgia. I had purposely put so many things out of my mind, and as I progressed from one self-innovation to the next, beginning with that modestly assumed British accent, I had left behind most of the people who were somehow part of the former self.

Then, that spring, I got sick. Cancer. No point going into the details. Years of joyous smoking had simply knocked me flat, and so in typical stiff-upper-lip fashion, I told myself, Well, nothing to be done. And I prepared to cool . . .

When Nancy Kissinger, who lives near me in Connecticut, found out I was planning to go for radiology treatments at a local clinic, she nearly went off her rocker—and Nancy is one of the most level-headed individuals I know. And a true friend. She and Henry had been having dinner with the Paul Markses—he had recently retired as president of Memorial Sloan-Kettering Cancer Center—and the next day Paul phoned and set me straight. Casey Ribicoff then took charge, taking me to Sloan sometimes twice a day for radiation, and visiting when I had to stay. She was an absolute lifesaver. It was an excruciating experience, not to mention goddamn unattractive. I was completely gaga. Or so I'm told.

But I did not die. Throughout the late summer and fall I got better. The cancer went away. Friends called. Oscar and Annette de la Renta, who live up the

road from me, in Kent, came often. I've known Oscar since the first month he arrived in New York from Paris, in 1962, when John Fairchild asked me to join them for lunch one day at the St. Regis. Henry Kissinger proved to be an extraordinary friend, too. I've never known anybody to have such a pure heart. When he was knighted by the queen a few years ago, he brought his mother. She and Nancy were invited to Ascot the next day, and his mother rode in a carriage. I thought that was wonderful. When Princess Diana came here in 1997, I asked her whom she wanted to lunch with, and she said Henry. Women are intrigued by his power. I would assume it's not his beauty. He does a kind of naïve chatter with women, and they just fall over. He offered me so much in the way of friendship when I was sick. He'd come on a Saturday morning and just sit here. One day he brought John McCain. An amazingly appealing man—and someone I had admired. His visit really lifted my spirits. And then two days later I received a letter from McCain's office and I thought, Isn't this sweet? But it was just a perfectly ordinary campaign letter sent to millions. Boy, if that didn't bring me down a peg.

Needless to say, I've had a lot of time to think about the people in my life, and the people who are no longer here. My father, of course. And my reach has widened. This has been the strange, unexpected blessing of a disease that would have killed me if I had not, for once, let my friends into my life. It has made me more open. And in that spirit, I am adding other voices—bits of dialogue, excerpts from diaries and letters—to the story from this point forward. I do so to finally fill in the blanks.

When I think about starting my life over, there are two things I would take with me. One is a small silver table in the shape of a tree trunk, with a top of petrified wood, that I found in Paris, and which stands next to my bed in my apartment in New York. It is the first thing I bought when I had enough money, and it has stayed with me, through various incarnations, through different periods, unchanged in my eye.

The other is a black-and-white photograph of a young man around the age of twenty. This is Edward Payson Guild. We met in New York in 1940, about

*Ed Guild
in Central Park.*

the time the snapshot was taken, and he, too, has stayed with me, unchanged, for more than half a century.

Ed wasn't my twin or other half. If there was a sexual attraction, it went unexpressed. He was simply my best friend. He was the first real friend I had. Initially roommates in that crowded West Side apartment, where each fellow had his own cereal box, Ed and I eventually moved into a place on Park Avenue South. He had come to New York straight from the New England prep school where his father was a master, and had taken a job downtown with W. R. Grace. So our backgrounds were as different as they could be. In the evenings, after work, we would join the thousands of young men—which New York seemed to specialize in then—going out to dinner or filling the sidewalks under the movie marquees. Afterward, back in our apartment, he would get in his bed and I'd get in mine, and we'd talk and talk. Philosophize.

I've known many people since with whom I could talk and go places and get drunk, but never again with that sense of discovery I found with Ed. My God, he made me go to hockey games. He wanted me to do everything with him.

He enlisted in the Marines in the spring of 1942, and died not long afterward, accidentally killed on basic maneuvers at Parris Island, South Carolina. After his body was returned to his family in Boston, his mother told me that the only thing personal he had on him was the last letter I had written. It was in the pocket of his fatigues.

Six months later, I entered the army.

2

Learning How to Lie

My mother, Ethyl Keyser Blass, came from Elm Grove, West Virginia, a small community outside Wheeling. She must have lived there with her two sisters and brother until she was in her early twenties, because I have a clipping from the local newspaper stating that she had been employed for several years by a Wheeling firm called Greer & Laing. Perhaps Ethyl enjoyed her work; perhaps she had no suitors until my father came along. That part of my mother's life is a

*With Ethyl
after the war.*

blank to me, but judging from this scrap of newsprint, I'd say that Ethyl wasn't in a hurry to enter matrimony.

The reason for the story, dated February 24, 1949, was to report that I had won a prize from Dan River Mills for a black-and-white gingham dress with a black patent leather belt, and to note that "although only a few folks 'round town actually know the young man, his mother is well remembered and her friends will rejoice in the signal [*sic*] honor that has come to her young son." The truth was that between September 1945, when I left the army, and early 1949, I had done little that was worth rejoicing about. Despite my eagerness to return to Seventh Avenue, I found the going curiously rough but illuminating. My former employer, David Crystal, had refused to take me back after his head designer complained that I was too ambitious. In a more powerful area of New York, such as banking or corporate law, a man like that would be laughed out of town. But in 1949, in the garment district—a place of Dreiserian amounts of soot and lint, crammed with hamburger dives, cigar shops, dress rack operators, models, and fabric salesmen, and controlled by manufacturers who'd arrive in their chauffeured Packards and Cadillacs—a designer couldn't afford to look too ambitious. He was expected to keep his head down, be grateful that he had been given the chance to design $79 copies of Dior dresses, and if he was the least bit lavender in his own tastes—shades of Danny Kaye in *Lady in the Dark*—then so much the better in the eyes of his bosses. They liked to think that their back-room designers were too preoccupied with making dresses to care about business. I can't say that I was fully aware of this attitude at twenty-three, my age when I left the army. But, according to the antidromic workings of Seventh Avenue—where everything goes against the normal—my Brooks Brothers blazer and sheen of junior executive confidence were *completely wrong.*

On the other hand, Anne Klein seemed to think I had no future at all. She took me on as a sketcher in her sportswear company—Varden, as it was then called—soon after the Crystal rejection, but fired me after less than a year, telling another manufacturer, "He has good manners but no talent." I remember thinking, Isn't that funny? She has no manners *and* no talent.* So, while jobless, I was not deeply wounded by Anne's remark. I must have recognized, with the resiliency of youth—and youth was so different in those days because of the Depression and then the war—that there would be other slights to endure. I still recall going for an interview, on a Sunday, at the home of a manufacturer and being asked to wait in the butler's pantry. This was right after the war and I still had on my uniform, freshly pressed, with the trousers tucked into the boots commando-style. I could hear cocktail chatter coming from the living room. After forty minutes, I left. I had thought the woman I was there to see would at least have had respect for the uniform. At the same time, though I wanted nothing more than to be a designer, I started casually telling people I met at parties (and presumed I would never meet again) that I was in advertising. I thought it sounded more serious and more attractive—but, above all, more real. Reality would have been a job where you actually entered through the front door. Clearly I harbored some self-consciousness about my chosen profession. But, honestly, at that point, it didn't feel like a profession. The manufacturers did their best to foster an atmosphere of contempt—based

---

*Years later we became good friends. Anne did have talent—for sportswear.

solely on their need to control a grim patch of hot dog stands and loft buildings. They hated the Italian garment makers for encroaching on their territory. They hated the unions and the Mafia for busting up their racket. But more than anything they hated the designers, because they knew that as soon as our talent was recognized, it would mean the end of their domination. Hence their need to keep us in the backroom, out of sight. I ought to say here that there was nothing homophobic about their bias. They hated the plainly talented Claire McCardell, too.

Eventually I got a job as an assistant at Anna Miller, whose brother, Maurice Rentner, had his own dress firm and wanted to see his sister in something respectable, though, like most figureheads in the business, Anna couldn't design clothes and had little taste. But I liked her. She was a small, blunt, white-haired dame straight out of Runyan, or Chandler. She was indeed "no paper flower," to quote the latter, and her habitual malapropisms kept the staff amused. If a model turned sulky or temperamental, Anna would bark, "Who the hell does she think she is, Sarah Bernhardt or Prima Donna?" Once, after returning from lunch at the Colony, she duly reported of another patron: "She just wore a simple suit and a foreskin over her shoulder."

1949, then, gave me the feeble beginnings of a career. Before starting at Anna Miller, I took my sister, Virginia, whom we called Gina, on a two-week spree to Paris—my prize from the Dan River Mills people for the gingham dress.* We saw the usual sights, filled up on the usual amounts of *pommes frites*, and I got to see my first French fashion shows: Dior, Fath, Schiaparelli. Then we came home. Never close as children, we were not likely to become so as adults. Though lively and good-looking, with soft brown hair, Gina had no interest in fashion and would soon settle into married life in upstate New York with an army officer named Stephen Camp, while I, who never wanted to marry, threw all my youthful energy into work and going out at night, where, with perfect deception, I used

---

*Though grateful to have the money (or free trip) that accompanied such awards, I mainly pursued them for the exposure. *Mademoiselle* would publish my entry for another contest, and I assume the West Virginia paper learned about the Dan River prize from the wire services. We *were* more innocent, then. Five thousand people, many of them art students and amateur designers, entered the *Chicago Tribune*'s annual American Fashion Competition in 1948, the year I won for a mustard wool jacket and blue skirt with a matching sealskin stole. That competition was held at the Plaza Hotel, and the winners each had their picture in the *Trib* the next morning—an inconceivable opportunity today.

my "advertising" line on unsuspecting strangers. So after the Paris trip—the first and last time my sister and I went anywhere together—our lives diverged, as they were destined to.

JOHN RICHARDSON: **Bill's a loner—very much a loner. I think he has a problem relating to people in that way. He's a marvelous friend, adored by his friends, too, but you have to leave the moves up to him, so he's in control of the situation. I adore Bill. I think he's sort of curiously faultless. There are not many shadows—well, there are shadows in the past and his family— but none in terms of his character.**

Ethyl's love for my father, a traveling hardware salesman named Ralph Aldrich Blass, was, like her need for secrecy, a mystery to me while I was grow-

With Gina and Ethyl on the roof of my mother's
Greenwich Village apartment.

ing up in Fort Wayne. That it ceased to be a mystery to me once I had moved away was only because, by the time I was in my twenties, I was engaged in some stealth of my own, so I had no curiosity about hers. This is a shame. Obviously my father's suicide, and its central unanswered question (*Why?*), go to the core of my isolated childhood and my sometimes futile—and not always pure—attempts later in life to find manly substitutes. In our family there was always a sense of something hidden, something unsaid, and I wish now I had pushed my mother to talk about these things. There might have been more understanding. But we just never talked about it. Not once.

I know nothing of the hows and whys that brought my parents together, and as I was barely five when my father died, all my information about him is secondhand. His family came from Angola, Indiana, was said to be well off, and had distinguished itself by producing one presidential cabinet member—my rich Chicago relative, my father's uncle, who, after serving as President Harrison's attorney general, went on to serve various Wrigleys.

At the time of my birth, on June 22, 1922, two years after my sister's, Ralph was earning his living traveling from one Midwestern town to the next, calling on hardware merchants. I have a dim olfactory memory of him—his pipe smell—but nothing else. Despite my mother's one attempt to ingratiate us with our Chicago relative, I never had the impression that his family felt anything but pride toward Ralph. After all, there could have been no shame in selling a commodity as basic to American life in the twenties as hardware. Similarly, I can't believe that money was the source of his troubles, or at least not money alone, as he died a full three years before the Depression, which, of course, made suicide epidemic. The best clue I have is my mother's silence, which she maintained to her grave, some thirty years later. What could be more unspeakable in a small town in that closeted era than mental illness, particularly if it was one of those dreaded illnesses like manic-depression—which I suspect my father had? And if untreated depression was the explanation, then what could be more terrifying to the mother of a young boy than the thought of openly discussing not only his father's suicide but also that of his father's father? Yes. I knew about my grandfather's suicide, too, but as with everything else about my family's history, it was with the ignorance of strangers.

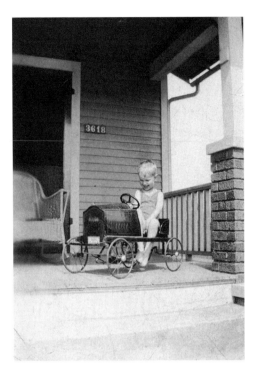

Ethyl did her best. While still in high school, I started calling her by her first name, or, if I wanted to tease her, then Ethyl Bert. We were close, despite—or because of?—our tacit withdrawal from the heavy subject of my father, and I felt that I could confide in her. So her approval of me was never in doubt. (Though Ethyl was wise enough to guess that I was different, she unconsciously turned a blind eye to the local Humberts who presented themselves to us as kindly father figures for me. More to this in a moment.) She possessed a natural goodness, was solidly built, polished in her manners and country handsomeness, and though she was rather stoic in her affections, embarrassed by kissing or hugging, she managed to make my sister and me feel that we were loved. She supported us on the income from a small annuity, the rental of our lake cottage, and money she earned by dressmaking, which she did, with decent success, in a spare room in our house on South Calhoun Street.

When I learned, a long time later, that our mother, a Fort Knox of discretion, had conducted love affairs in that modest little house, I was shocked and

in a way pleased that she had kept even this hidden from us. I forget now who my informant was; not Ethyl, surely. But I was to have other clues that Ethyl was not as passive as she appeared, when during the war she came east to live, and in that strange city made new friends, found work she liked as a museum guide, and often went out to dinner with Bob Tompkins's wife, Bunny. When Bob and I came home from Europe, it was Ethyl who offered to transcribe his field diary of our secret army work. She needed a magnifying glass to read the Lilliputian text—kept small to avoid the notice of the brass. But it was the sort of patient work for which she was well qualified, and I think it made her feel closer to me.

To say, now, that growing up fatherless did not affect me would be a blatant untruth. I'm sure it accounts for my rather tendentious views about family—chiefly, who needs it? Some of us *do* arrive in the world with the feeling of being separated, which isolation, especially the isolation of the Midwest, gradually hones, at least for the hopeful among us, into self-reliance. When I arrived in New York at seventeen, I had no sense of family, no sense of religion, and very little idea of what it meant to be a man. The war would settle most of these questions. That I have never bothered to look too closely into my family's history is somewhat surprising, given that on my nightstand at this moment (January 2002) is the new Anthony Blunt biography, and out on the bench in the dining room, waiting like patients, are more personal histories to be examined. I don't know whether it's a weakness or a virtue to live so comfortably in the present, but it does seem to me that I was in some sense inured to my past. Then life took over. The east-bound train, the fast receding summer of Ohio and Pennsylvania, and then the dark tunnel into Manhattan. After 1940, life just started to speed up.

ADOLFO: **I saw Bill before I actually knew who he was. I was coming out of St. Patrick's one morning and I saw this man walking down Fifth Avenue. He was the best-looking man I'd ever seen. Then we met a little while after that. Bill was the person who gave me the money to start my business, in 1962. He gave me the first $10,000, and then I was able to raise more from some clients. I paid him back within three months. But hardly anyone knows what he did for me, and he never wanted anyone to know. When one of my models died suddenly, he handed me a check at the funeral and said, "Give this to her daughter."**

I've always had a problem with money—not the making of it but the idea of it. When I was first living in New York and had no money, I always acted as if I did. I bought the best clothes I could afford; in those days, Brooks. With a little more money, I moved up to Lord, a custom shop then in vogue. And up and up until I finally hit London, Savile Row, H. Huntsman—tailors to countless British gentlemen—and, my God, if a man doesn't have his insecurities knocked out of him by that point, there's no hope for him.

But now that I have money, I'm always afraid of losing it. I recognize that this fear, and its constant companion of self-invention, are holdovers from the Depression, when you always felt in danger of losing your social position—though, in my family, the danger was academic since we had already slipped prominently into the negative category with my father's suicide. This is perhaps an exaggeration, but

In New York: I already had the accent and the cigarette.

I've never shared in the illusion that the miseries of the Depression drew people to-gether like a roaring college bonfire. That was the reality of the Second World War; the Depression isolated and trapped people in their private shame. I didn't realize, then, how much energy goes into keeping up a perfect front, which shame neces-sarily entails. And as I spent most of my youth in a continuous trance of movies and fashion magazines, I was in a sense already in a happier place; I hadn't yet escaped to New York, but in my mind I had.

The difficulty comes, of course, when the need to keep up appearances suddenly veers into an adult-size quest for acceptance—and on the scale that New York has to offer. Then you start inventing various guises for yourself, covering up in order to keep up. It's an interesting process, enlightening in many ways, but not *lightening*. Because you never feel comfortable in the character you've created. You're always improvising, always seeking better forms of cover.*

*In one guise or another, I remain William Ralph Blass. But so many nicknames: Blassy (in high school); Willy (suitably WW II); Bilbo (favored by both Jacques Tiffeau and Jerry Zipkin, a.k.a. Tiff and Zip); Billy Buck (the choice of Texans); the Frenchy Guillaume, or Guy (par Louise Grunwald); and briefly, in the fifties, the show-stopping Bootsie Blass. So many nicknames, so many periods. But a coincidence?

LEARNING HOW TO LIE

Inevitably I was drawn to people whose backgrounds were different than mine. The most resplendent by far was Baron Nicolas de Gunzburg. Tall, thin, aloof, with a basset hound expression that blended with a droll wit, Niki was serving a perfunctory term as editor of *Town & Country* when we first met in the late forties, and would soon become an editor at *Vogue*. It was Niki who introduced me to Vreeland—or, rather, shoved her in my general direction, at Anna Miller, since Diana was not then in the habit of coming to Seventh Avenue. On the day she did arrive (picture her: the raven hair, the pitched-back walk, the flaring cigarette), she brushed past the old boys in the front office, ignoring everyone, and announced: "I hear you have a young Englishman in your backroom. I must meet him." Vreeland could always be counted on for getting things slightly wrong, though perhaps for the right reasons. Niki, however, proved to be a greater influence on me. His family had been enormously rich in the twenties in Paris, and Niki himself might have been so if his father, a financier to the czar and then to Cesar Ritz, hadn't died before telling him where his inheritance was. He spent his life, and a small fortune, looking for the money. In spite of this, Niki lived well, disconcertingly well, and during the years that I knew him, which was until his death in 1981, his style remained as elegant as it was unvaried. He always wore the same type of dark suit, white shirt, black tie, black shoes, and everything he owned was made for him. Even his ties were custom, by Knize in Vienna. I went to Knize once. It really is a snotty joint. But the rest of Niki's clothes were made by obscure tailors somewhere. He had the security to do that, whereas I needed the security of Lobb shoes, the right tailor, and all that.

Financial security doesn't bring a lessening of money consciousness, not when it is rooted in the Depression and especially not after it becomes attached to the trellises of New York. This image, naturally, suggests an enthusiasm for social advancement. And I've had my share, and even been guilty of sounding the occasional Parnassian snort of disapproval. I admit it. But this story, now from the early seventies, involves a wholly different view—when John Weitz wrote me into his novel *The Value of Nothing* as one Philip Ross, a social-climbing fashion designer who brings home stray Marines and eventually gets bumped off by one. I'm afraid the Marine cliché is not the book's only flaw, but never mind. John and I were great pals—and remained so, despite the fuss that erupted, for another

*With the designer John Weitz, and the
fashion editor Sally Kirkland in the sixties.*

decade. He had been in the OSS during the war and, as he never tired of mentioning, had grown up in privilege in Berlin before the Nazis. The two of us spent many twilight hours drinking on my Sutton Place terrace, where John came to escape from his second wife, the fashion editor Eve Orton, and I was best man at his third marriage, to the beautiful Susan Kohner, then a Hollywood star.

I didn't believe for a minute John's protestations that Ross wasn't me, but neither did I care. I remember Eugenia Sheppard, the saucy (and pint-size) fashion editor of the *New York Herald Tribune*, being furious about it, though.

"How can you speak to him after something like this?" Eugenia demanded, her blond curls shaking just below the vicinity of my sternum.

"Well," I replied, "I *am* described very attractively."

I'd learned early not to show vulnerability. And, of course, it's always the lodgers who lodge the complaint of reinvention, which has been in practice in this country, as far as I can tell, since the *Mayflower*. Steven Kaufmann, who, at ninety, is not only one of the oldest people I know, but also my oldest friend, often chides me for my stuffier views about money. But then, as a Pittsburgh department store Kaufmann, he had it, and I didn't. For me, money implied a knowledge—no, better, an experience—that had been denied to me growing up, and which I felt I could mediate with discipline and hard work. And, curiously, I think that much of my sanity—and, later, success—on Seventh Avenue came from consciously appearing to be outside the penny-ante game, though I knew where every penny was going and what was selling. When I had my own business and would travel anywhere—usually with Tom Fallon, who did the PR, and Gail Levenstein, who handled licenses (and who shared my sense of humor)—we always went first class. The best hotels, etc. I'm sure I overdid things.

At the same time, I have a well-attested abhorrence of confrontation. I couldn't have stood the sort of garmento business partner who'd say, "Why do you need two hundred pairs of Manolo Blahnik shoes?" And finding someone who thought the way I did, and could deal with the shenanigans of Seventh Avenue, would have been a mean feat.* So I never had a partner, and many times I paid dearly for this. But I never wanted it any other way.

STEVEN KAUFMANN: **Even when he had no money, Bill lived beautifully. He's always managed. But he never had a clue about money, not even to this day. I often think that when I cool, which could be any hour, he'll call up Casey Ribicoff and say, "I can't get over it, he didn't have a penny." I can hear him.**

In 1971, thirty-two years after I thought I had left Fort Wayne for good, I returned for a fashion show at a local store—duly hot-footed by a reporter from *Women's Wear Daily*. As Fort Wayne had always loomed as distantly in my background as the Japanese sun—no more than an exotic blur—this reporter evi-

*The notable exception was Ben Shaw, who financed the firms of Donald Brooks and Jane Derby. A man as charismatic as he was intelligent, Shaw and his wife, Miriam, had a complicated relationship. She was one of Balenciaga's few intimates, and he made things for her, including corsets and undergarments, that he did for no one else. But correctness ended with Shaw. More typical was the garmento I once overheard say to my assistant: "Blass is always being photographed with a cigarette. I don't want him photographed, because he's not going to last long the way he smokes. Better that no one knows what he looks like if we have to get a new designer." That was in 1968.

Back in the cornfields of Indiana, 1971.

dently sensed a great opportunity to flush me out. Or, as he put it, "to get to the bottom of some Blass myths."

No, I had not played high school football. No, I had never been married; this said as I tossed him a distracting bone: "I was once engaged to marry but I can't remember her name." A lie—to the engagement part and thus to the other.

The reporter didn't know what he was up against. Ethyl's boy wasn't going to drop his guard for a casual marauder. But now it is 2002, another thirty years has passed, and I find myself in the unfamiliar position of wanting to tell the truth. Why now? Because I've realized, perhaps belatedly, that my story—the story of Ethyl, Ralph, the mashed potato sandwiches, the magnifying glass on the page— has its own unblemishable grandeur.

So it does me no harm, now, to return to the earlier part of the narrative . . .

When I said that Ethyl unconsciously turned a blind eye to the local Humberts appearing as father figures, I meant just that. She didn't know—nor, in that naïve era, would she have suspected—that some of the men who offered to take me out for Sunday ice cream or to a ball game actually had other objectives in mind. I was eight when the first incident happened, and while I can't claim that these experiences put me for or against homosexuality (nor would I bother to), I knew that this was not love. I wanted a father figure, but more than that, I wanted someone to talk to. And these were not men who talked.

Paradoxically, I've spent the whole of my adult life talking a blue streak about books, fashion, food, dogs, decorating, society, what so-and-so said at last night's party . . . And I have not stopped talking since the day I arrived in New York, some sixty-two years ago.

3

Willy with His Hat Down Low

I can see now that I have grossly underplayed my role in the Second World War. A book has recently come my way—*Ghost Army of World War II*, by a fellow named Jack Kneece, one of several authors bringing out books about my army unit—and the picture he presents of me outwitting the German General von Ramcke and his *forty thousand* troops at Brest truly is amazing, if not one for the record books. I am indeed *one* of the American soldiers whose decoy lines of inflatable rubber tanks fooled Von Ramcke in August 1944, allowing Patton to slip past and bowl on to Paris. But I'm afraid Mr. Kneece gives me far too much warrior credit. You'd think from the play I receive that Ike and I alone had won the war.

Of course, it is interesting that so many men in my outfit went on to distinguish themselves after the war. In our group were the painter Ellsworth Kelly, the photographer Art Kane, and George Diestel, who was to design sets for the movies; as well as several hundred other artists, designers, and commercial illustrators, most of them young and straight out of the art schools and advertising agencies of New York and Philadelphia when they joined the 603rd Camouflage Battalion.

So there was definitely something novel about a military outfit composed entirely of creative people. We supposedly had the highest average IQ in the

33

army, 119. I couldn't swear to this. I spent most of my war inflating dummy tanks and dreaming up marvelous new uses for chicken feathers. The rest of the time I was in a bubble—a bubble of delight. I know this is a strange thing to say, given that we weren't exactly in the most delightful place on earth—the French mud with German shells exploding around us. I remember standing on a hill one morning, right after we'd landed in Normandy, as 3,500 Allied bombers flew over our heads. You don't forget a sight like that. But here is how I know that I was in a bubble: For years, whenever someone asked me if I was in Paris on Liberation Day—and, let's face it, it's not a question one gets a lot—I would smile and say, "Why, yes." Then I'd describe the whole jubilant scene. The poppies. The waving French schoolchildren. Now I discover, in the course of working on this book, that I wasn't in Paris at all—but in a tent, in Brest, in the rain. I had imagined the whole thing. We got to Paris, eventually . . . two weeks later. But that's what I mean by a bubble. I wasn't aware of anything except being happy.

Left to right: Paul LaHive, Bob Tompkins, and myself in France.

The fact that I am smiling idiotically in every picture taken of me during the war is another indication that I couldn't have given Von Ramcke much personal trouble. You see, for me, the war didn't represent the hardship that it did for my friend Bob Tompkins, who, after all, had a wife and a baby at home, or that it might have for Ed Boccia, another fellow in my outfit who, like Bob, had just graduated from Pratt. For me, the three and half years that I spent in the army represented absolute freedom. I was truly on my own for the first time in my life. So, naturally, in that exuberant state of mind, I didn't always notice how bad things were.

FROM BOB TOMPKINS'S WAR DIARY, AUGUST 24, 1944: **Moved up 500 yards to new area and set up 10 tanks. Willy and I set up our tent with our feet sticking out in the pouring down rain and pass out at 3:00 A.M.**

ED BOCCIA: **Blass was always cheerful. We could be up day and night, night and day, so that you don't know whether the sun's coming up or going down. You get pretty grumpy. But Blass never got grumpy, no matter how hard it got. He always had this big smile and these big white teeth—as if he was at a party somewhere.**

Unless you forget where we were, my party face couldn't have always been welcomed. The moment our sergeant gave lung to his standard reveille line—"Drop your cocks and grab your socks!"—I was up and outside, while the other guys were still stumbling around and trying to get connected. I think that was a time when they would have liked to have wiped the shit-eating grin off my face.

Today, of course, there is a great deal of nostalgia for the war; I get calls all the time from journalists asking me about it, even though, as I say, my part was very small. And I don't know if someone can appreciate what it meant to a kid who had only just left the farm, so to speak—who, really, in many ways, was still a mama's boy—to suddenly be among men, literally thousands of them, in a life-and-death situation. Have you ever seen those photographs of troopships,

July 1944. I am with Bob Tompkins in an apple orchard in Normandy.

crammed with guys lying stem to stern on the deck like bathers at Coney Island, except they have on fatigues and about fifty pounds of gear? That is my other picture of the war—a world entirely of men.

Until then, except for that brief period in New York, I'd lived exclusively with women—my mother, Gina, and my mother's younger sister, Anna. And I see, now, that as my career accelerated, in the mid-fifties, I began, again, to spend more and more time with women. But in those intervening years, between leaving Indiana and establishing my name in New York, it is really a man's story. Of a boy coming of age, yes; but also, in my case, of recognizing that the qualities I admired most in men—among them, loyalty, responsibility, a love of order, and certainly courage under fire—were not ones I associated with the shrill and effeminate world of fashion. I am not saying that such qualities cannot be found there; only that, in the period when I was forming opinions about manhood, they were not evident to me. I know, too, that in making such a statement I am bound to be criticized, since I have lived most of my life in a contradictory position—with one part of myself safely in the closet and the other out and up to all kinds of things. But it is a contradiction I can live with, among others. Manhood, whether it wears a hard face or an eye-catching negligee, may still be manhood, but at a certain point it comes down to a decision of conduct. For me, after the war, there was no choice. I would always feel more comfortable in a heterosexual world than a homosexual one. And, paradoxically, I think this sense of familiarity, acquired during the worst of circumstances, subsequently gave me greater ease and insight into the lives of the women I dressed.

Ed Boccia: **You didn't know what Bill was, sexually. He was somewhere in the middle, I guess. I don't remember anyone teasing him. And you've got to consider that in our battalion, except for the high noncoms—the sergeants and the officers— we were all kids out of art school and we had more sense than that. It wasn't: "I'm a tough guy, let's punch this kid out." God, we were really not fighters.**

Airborne: One of our inflatable tanks.

I enlisted in the army's camouflage unit in the fall of 1942, and went straight to basic training at Fort Meade, Maryland. The 603rd was one of four noncombat units that were part of a phantom division called the Twenty-third Headquarters Special Troops. I say phantom because throughout the war—indeed, for years after—only a handful of brass and the eleven hundred enlisted men involved knew of its existence. Our identity was kept secret for the simple reason that we were posing as other Allied troops in order to fool the enemy. That's what we were doing at Brest—pretending to be Patton's armor, the Fifteenth Tank Battalion. Except, that instead of his Shermans, we had rubber ones that we inflated at night and left in his same tank tracks. We even had ways of faking tank fire and noise, which the men in our sonic unit blasted all night long at the Germans. So when Von Ramcke looked the next morning through the haze and battle smoke with his field glasses, he thought he was seeing Patton's forces. In a matter of hours he would have known it was a ruse, but by then, Patton had attacked somewhere else, and we and our portable dummy tanks had vanished. We did this sort of thing in twenty-one engagements, often simulating troops ten and fifteen times our size, right up to the crossing of the Rhine.

While at Meade, I met Tompkins, who had been headed for a career in advertising. At nineteen, he was a year younger than I, but with his confident manner and dashing good looks, set off by a thin Errol Flynn mustache, he somehow seemed more worldly. Also, he was married, to the lovely Bunny—whom he called Babe—and the three of us soon started going around together.

BOB TOMPKINS: **Bill looked athletic, but he wasn't. I remember once we were coming into Penn Station on a weekend furlough. And, you know, as trains come into a station, they slow down and if you want to get off a moving train, you have to jump with it. Bill didn't. He just stepped out and rolled over a couple of times. Bunny was waiting for us in the lobby, amidst thousands of service people, and I said, "Bill will be along in a minute." Then he came running across the floor of Penn Station, hollering, "Bunny, dear, I'm sorry, but I fell off the train." He had his hat pulled down over his eyes.**

With Bob and Bunny Tompkins, Christmas 1943.

Although our secret nighttime movements behind front lines made it un-likely that we'd ever have to shoot anybody, the army nonetheless expected us to know how to use a carbine. And to drill, of course. Where I fell down completely, in the eyes of the army, was driving. A car would have been way beyond our means in Fort Wayne. So I hadn't learned to drive—and it soon became clear to both the army and myself, as I lurched disturbingly around the motor pool in one of its training Jeeps, that I never would. And, in fact, never did. (It seems relevant here to mention that the only thing more remarkable than my driving record is that for eighteen years, begining in the mid-seventies, I endorsed a line of Lincoln Conti-nentals for the Ford Motor Company without knowing how to operate one—a fact I finessed with Ford executives by saying, when asked if I'd like to take a new model for a spin around Dearborn, "No, I'll just sit in it and get a feel.")

The cross section of men in my outfit was fascinating. Early on, the army decided that our creative ranks lacked sufficient brawn, so it brought in men from places like Pennsylvania and West Virginia—really tough guys who had been coal miners and bartenders. I heard country and western music for the first time in my life; at one end of the barracks you'd hear Beethoven's Third and at the other, "Pistol Packin' Mama." Certainly, on the whole, the enlisted men were brighter than the officers. I recall two: a dark-haired, swarthy, extraordinarily beautiful fellow named Taber de Polo. Taber never wore a coat in the winter. All day long he'd just stroll around in a shirt. Very macho. The other was a blond beauty from the South named Clark Battle Fitzgerald. An absolute pain in the ass. I loved the fact that, while both were straight out of central casting, they were such opposites. During the war, Bob drove for another officer, a Lieutenant Gray, who had been Helen Hayes's stage manager and whose general slowness earned him the sobriquet "Grandmother." He talked like this: "*Ohh*, fuh *h-e-a-v-e-n's* sake, Blass, *w-h-a-t* are you *d-o-in'* now." I thought he'd never get the words out.

By late January 1944, when our outfit was sent to Tennessee for further training, most of us assumed we'd never get overseas. It wasn't that any of us was in such a hurry to get into the war, but the waiting you do in the army makes you think that any place is better than where you are. So, until we received our orders to go to England, in late April, we were stuck in the deepest woods of Tennessee, with absolutely no place to go. On our only weekend furlough, Bunny drove down from New York, and the three of us went over to a little town called McMinnville, where there was a hotel.

Bob now swears the Sedberry Hotel was a brothel, but I have my doubts. *Certainly* the Sedberry was seeing considerable action from the nearby army post—and it was an incredible novelty to sleep in a real feather bed with real sheets after months of hard cots. What I chiefly remember about the place is the food. Now, I know a lot about food. I've eaten in some swell joints, and I've convinced myself that I can remember everything I ever ate, even as a child. The summer fruit pies we had in Indiana. The absolute beauty of the cole slaw. My aunt Anna's chicken and dumplings. So rich and delicious.

But I think the food in McMinnville was the best I've ever tasted. I know this because when you're in the army you think you're never going to get another meal again. You're always starved. And it gets worse in war, because then you're not only starving, you're also tired, cold, and dirty. Everything acquires a kind of relative-state importance, food especially. I used to wonder, when we finally got to England and were quartered next to some British soldiers, how they had the strength to fight on the slop they were fed. We weren't faring much better with our shit on a shingle, but it was a luxury compared to what those poor British Tommies got.

The notebook I kept during the war.

So I've savored the memory of the McMinnville weekend for a reason. The owner of the inn had roast turkey on the menu, with corn bread and chestnut stuffing. She had sweet potatoes done in a casserole, with dates and brown sugar and a little rum. There was hand-cranked ice cream, peach and strawberry, and she had tins of cakes, in big square pans . . . beautiful sheet cakes with caramel or coconut frosting. It was another world to us.

In fact, we would eat nothing better again until the late summer of 1944, in Normandy, when we were living in tents between hedgerows and could barter with our G.I. cigarettes and chocolate for fresh eggs, bread, and maybe a lump of butter. And even here, taste had a delicious relative potency, when our K-ration jam hit the fresh bread . . .

We landed at Omaha Beach in July 1944. Bob had come over a few weeks earlier with a corps of drivers. I arrived with what was referred to as the "residual" forces, in a gusting storm, and had to climb down nets on the side of the ship to go ashore. My first look of France, a country I'd known only through the glittery pages of fashion magazines, was of bombed-out villages, dead farm animals abuzz with flies, and *miles* of military vehicles backed up on the narrow roads. On our way up to the Brittany peninsula, we passed a headless cow dangling thirty feet in the air from a charred tree. There were bomb craters everywhere, and everywhere ghostly villages. Truckloads of German POW's rolled past us, going east.

It amazes me, now, to think that for four or five months in 1944, before we moved east ourselves and took part in the last big offensives of the war—the Battle of the Bulge and the crossing of the Rhine—our little outfit was a Michelin of remote French villages and back roads. Much later, in the seventies, after two decades' worth of going to Paris for the collections, eating French food, and putting up generally with French snottiness, I told people I was bored with France, and went more to London, a city I've loved without reserve. But for that summer and fall, I and the thousand or so guys in the Twenty-third covered the countryside like natives. The practical thing was to travel at night, when we wouldn't be noticed by spies, and of course this not only meant that we were getting to sleep at two or three o'clock in the morning—often in a tent or mud hut leaking with rain—but also that we were traveling in total darkness, because of black-out restrictions.

Although our work kept us just behind the front lines and therefore out of immediate danger, we experienced the same disorienting effects of sleeplessness and going for weeks without a bath as other soldiers did. With this difference: We were impersonating them and they didn't know it. Before every operation, we'd have to switch all our insignia markings, including those on our Jeeps and shoulder patches, to reflect the unit we were simulating. Usually this was a straightforward process—a fresh coat of paint and a few minutes with a needle and thread—but in the confusion before the Bulge, before it was decided that we would impersonate the Seventy-fifth Infantry Division, we changed our identity four times. I don't know if being part of an invisible force made us luckier than the soldier in the foxhole, or if by being known he was luckier because his bravery was recognized. I do know that when Patton drove by some of our troops, shortly after Brest, and saw men with so many different arm patches, he was furious—presumably, taking them for laggards.

But I've never really given the matter of recognition much thought. For me, the experience of the war satisfied needs that had gone unmet in my own life. Brotherhood. The feeling that I could survive anything. That was the only kind of recognition I wanted.

With Tompkins and George Vandersluis in Normandy.

With no more armies to simulate after the Allies pushed across the Rhine in March, our unit was given the grim task of protecting nearly 100,000 displaced persons—mostly from marauding Russians and Poles. I've never seen more sad and desperate people in my life; the Russians would steal a bicycle right out from under a person, or come at him with pitchforks. It just made us all want to get home that much more badly. Finally, on May 19, we received the word, and slowly began moving west, passing through areas that were completely in ruins, until we reached Le Havre on June 22, my twenty-third birthday.

The next day, at 7:25 P.M., on June 23, our troopship, the *Leonard O. H. Ernst*, pulled up anchor and began its nine-day voyage across the Atlantic. Like every other ship going out, it was crammed, the guys agreeing to sleep in shifts—"hot-bunking," as it was called—if it meant they would get home sooner.

At 6 A.M. on July 2, we saw the Virginia coast.

At 10 A.M., we docked at Newport News. Before boarding a train that would eventually take us to New York, I sent a telegram to my mother and sister, and Bob sent one to Bunny.

BUNNY TOMPKINS: **Around 11 P.M. on July 2, I received the telegram that Bob was coming home. I was in the house alone with a seven-month-old baby and nobody to yell to. So I called Bob's folks first and then I called Ethyl. On the first ring she picked up and said, "We got our telegram this afternoon but we didn't want to spoil the surprise for you." Then she said, "They'll probably come home together, so why don't you plan to come over to our apartment for dinner." So the three of us were sitting there having dinner when we heard the elevator door open and somebody clear his throat. And Ethyl said, "That's Bill." And Gina and I said, "Oh, come on." And the next second the doorbell rang and it was Bill and Bob. It was the early evening of July 5, 1945.**

4

All Around the Moon

The English have such an amazing attitude about sex. Of course, everybody knows about the manners of the English. But the absolute civility of their upper classes toward anything that's the least bit in flagrante delicto is something I've always noticed about the British. They simply accept the possibility that a married man can have a love affair with a girl as easily as a guy and still keep his wife happy. Or vice versa. I know of many couples in New York who have a similar understanding; even by all appearances a successful marriage. But whenever I read a biography or memoir of someone once known to that small, glamorous, limited world of England in the thirties, I am struck by how differently their educated class views sex.

For instance, let's imagine that a few close friends are staying at someone's beautiful country house, and it's night. All of a sudden the bedroom doors are left unlocked; somebody sneaks in and does a nice little bit of nooky, and then goes back to his or her own room. The next morning everybody is perfectly fine about it. No terrible scenes and, at the same time, no undue skulking. Which is my point: When it comes to sex, the English are discreet—*and* open.

I started going to London a lot in the sixties when I was designing my men's collections. Today, hardly anyone remembers how revolutionary men's fashion was then—just the fact that Carter Burden and John Lindsay, the mayor of New York—men obviously with conservative tastes but also better things to do than shop—would go over to Bonwit's to get the latest windowpane plaid suit with high armholes. I wasn't the first American women's designer to do men's clothes—John Weitz was, in 1964—but I was the first to come out of the upper end of the business, in 1967. So I was going to London, to pick up ideas.

In those days I tended to have more confirmed opinions about things than I do now; not that I've ever lacked for something to say, and certainly if there's one thing I know how to do it's to deflate a situation. Just let the hot air out . . . I remember once taking Louise Grunwald with me to Zurich, to look at fabrics at Abraham—which, as you may know, has the most beautiful fabrics in the world—and here is Louise, in the middle of Abraham, having a situation I would say is comparable to Gloria Guinness collapsing in her seat at Balenciaga, when he introduced the maillot. Louise is in ecstasy. "Oh, the fabrics . . . *oh!*"

Finally she grabbed some lace I was looking at and she held it up to herself and said, "Oh, Guy, what will you do with this?"

"Probably fuck it up," said Guy.

But for a while I was rather set in my opinions. I was very aware, you see, of wanting approval—all kinds, though none more than fashion approval. After all, I wasn't the innovator that Balenciaga was. Women like Gloria didn't fall to pieces when they saw my clothes. They just put them on and wore them. And don't forget this was the period when I was living in the penthouse with the lacquered tortoiseshell walls, at 444 East 57th Street, the one whose self-conscious masculine swank John Richardson had spotted when he went there to visit Bat Stewart . . . Anyway, one day in 1968, Nora Ephron came over to interview me for an article she was doing for the *New York Times* magazine about the explosion in my men's business. I don't remember how long Nora was in my closet, but she had a good look around—sniffed everything out. Then she wrote: "He owns 25 tailored suits, three dinner jackets (one of them lightweight for dancing), several dozen pairs of Lobb shoes, and 12 overcoats, two of them fur-lined . . . When Blass goes to London, he packs only his underwear, because he goes straight to Kilgour, French and Stanbury* for the five suits he ordered on his last trip to London."

*My tailor at the time.

*Hitting the town
with Louise Grunwald
in the sixties.*

My God. All the way from "fuck it up" to Kilgour, French and Stanbury! Talk about needing approval.

But then I was forty-six years old—already *ancient* by today's star standards—and on the verge of finally having my own business after twenty years of working for the same two men on Seventh Avenue. I was going out nearly every night, to one party or another, and rarely getting home before midnight; yet, whether I realized it or not at the time, I was doing some of the best work of my career—snappy minidresses and fur-trimmed coats that were being photographed on girls like Candice Bergen and Marisa Berenson in *Vogue*. I knew every important fashion editor in town, and I had begun to travel to other American cities and meet women like Lynn Wyatt in Houston, Emma Andrews and Sally Debenham in San Francisco, or Mary Landon in Omaha, gals who influenced the taste in their towns and, of course, helped me to become known outside New York.

KENNETH JAY LANE: **Bill was so laid-back. He was better than he realized, in a funny way. He was more talented than he realized. Yet he brought something to American fashion that nobody else did—something fresh and sportive. He *got* the American woman. Of course, he got ideas from Norman Norell, who did the cashmere and paillette thing. But Bill's things were much more wearable. Diana Vreeland once said after a Norell show: "Oh, my God, those clothes are so beautiful. But do you know anyone who wears them?" But people wore and wore and wore Bill's clothes.**

Laid-back—and constantly moving toward the next phase, the next place, the next experience. Then . . . *Got to go!* This is the perhaps strangest pattern that I've noticed in going back over my life: how great was my concentration for my career, but practically nil for anything else. Once I settled into Anna Miller, which eventually, in the late fifties, was folded into Maurice Rentner, I stayed there, patiently boring away like a tree beetle. All in good time, I told myself. And in time it did happen—I made it through. But the pattern of the rest of my life was to experience things in short, incremental bursts of interest. Then move on. Cuba. Fire Island. Southampton. It was always the same: the declarative strike, followed by the peremptory withdrawal.

JOHN WEITZ: **Bill absorbs quickly the things that please him, and drops them at the slightest hint of their becoming déclassé. When Susan and I were honeymooning, he said, "Take my house." He had rented a house in Southampton from Carrie Munn, who was the last wife of the socialite Orson Munn. So we stayed there. This was in 1964. But Bill had dumped Southampton by then.**

Only my career, apparently, was exempt from this Peter Pan approval system, as were certain friends—plainly Stevie and the deeply missed Glenn Bernbaum and Louise, who was Louise Savitt, then married to the tennis star Richard

Savitt and working at *Vogue*, when we first met in the late fifties. Everything else I subjected to a much harsher editing process that involved the intricate business of reinvention and seeking better forms of cover. It applied to rooms and places and, inevitably, to romantic love. But since this chapter already has the feel of a joy ride—with a purpose, mind you—let's return for a moment to London . . .

It is now 1985 and I am with my driver, Ian Wood, and we are heading toward the antiques shops on the Pimlico Road. The apartment at 444 has been cleared of its tortoiseshell and oriental chintz, and on one long white wall now hangs a huge trompe l'oeil painting of muskets and standards by the Dutch painter Jacobus Biltius. Below it is an Irish side table set between two Georgian globes. The car turns onto Pimlico Road.

NINA GRISCOM: **He goes into a place knowing exactly what he wants. I've never seen the man waver. He'll tell me, "That's good. Or, that's got guts." And you know that if it has guts it's going to**

*Glenn Bernbaum,
Duane Hampton, and me,
antiquing in Belgium.
Mark Hampton is behind
the camera.*

**wind up in his house or warehouse. He likes garden sculpture—
he was into that before anyone else. And he doesn't like long
explanations. He wants it in a nutshell.**

The person who really opened my eyes about pictures as well as furniture
is John Richardson. I started shopping with him in London in the early eighties. I
don't remember when we first met. I didn't know him when he was at Christie's. I
didn't know him when he was at Knoedler. More than likely we met in the seventies through Kitty Miller. People had warned me about him: "My God, he's so dangerous. He says the most wicked things." But I found I never enjoyed traveling with
anyone as much as I did John. He's so knowledgeable. He'll see a chair and say,
"Isn't that funny, it belonged to so-and-so." Of course, the person is obscure as you
can imagine. But John forgets nothing. I remember him saying once, "Oh, that belonged to Lord Beacon. You know who he is of course? He's the 'Bathtub Baby.'"

"What do you mean?" I said.

"Oh, he was the child who was conceived in a bathtub. His mother had
taken a bath right at the same time as Lord So-and-So, and conceived in the
bathtub."

I mean, you get information from John that you'd never hear from anyone else.

He took me to the less obvious places in London, and in Amsterdam and
Brussels. And I loved the way he would go into a shop. John never goes in lan-
guidly. He pounces in. Grabs the first thing that appeals to him. No preliminaries.
He says, "How much is this?" I always say, "No, I'm just looking, thank you . . . "
Honestly, I learned so much from him. He knows the history, the scandal, the truth
about everyone.

JOHN RICHARDSON: **Mica Ertegun arranged for me to advise Bill
on what drawings to collect. I think he thought, Oh, God. He
probably had reservations. But we got on extremely well . . . Bill
is enormously quick. He has a fairly instant reaction to whatever
it might be or it's: "Let's get out of here, kid . . ." There was no
pretending he knew more than he did. He was completely**

frank—either he knew or he didn't know. And he never, ever haggled. I haggle my head off, but I think he found it a bit tacky.

I'm often asked how I got to know so many people, especially when I was first coming along in the early fifties and didn't have any social connections to speak of. The answer is simple: I was interested in what they had to say. I'd be invited by Kitty Miller to one of her parties—Kitty was a grande dame, not beautiful but always beautifully turned out in Mainbocher or Givenchy—and I'd get to talking with her husband, Gilbert, who was a theatrical producer. His friends didn't ask him about the theater. God knows Kitty didn't care. She didn't give a damn. But I was fascinated by his early stories. Ask a man about his business and he loves talking about it.

C. Z. GUEST: **Now, Kitty told me that when Bill first came to New York he worked for Anna Miller and then Maurice Rentner, and when one of them became ill, he behaved so well. And coming from Kitty that was some compliment, because she used to have a tongue like an asp. *Oooh!* And you know she was the daughter of Jules Bache. I mean, if she liked you, great. She certainly liked Bill. And Kitty was a hell of a snob.**

Of course, Seventh Avenue was a business like any other, and there was money to be made. In those days, the business was divided among three groups: the $12.95 dress manufacturers, like Jonathan Logan, who represented the lowest price (and about half the total market); the sportswear designers, like McCardell, Tom Brigance, and Bonnie Cashin, who were doing innovative (but not inexpensive) things in denim and cotton; and the "cloakies," the expensive coat and suit makers, like Ben Zuckerman, Originala, and Mangone, who followed what was coming out of Paris.

I started going to Paris for Anna Miller around 1953 when the head designer, Earl Luick, decided he'd had taken it on the chin long enough, and went back to designing for Hollywood. Like the other Seventh Avenue firms, we paid a caution to the French houses that entitled us to buy a certain number of original

Kitty Miller in her Park Avenue apartment. Behind her is Goya's Boy in Red.

styles, which we'd modify back in New York for our customers. You ought to have seen the Paris showings. I don't think anyone realized, until Balenciaga suddenly closed his doors in 1968, that we were witnessing the end of a world. Everybody sat on bentwood salon chairs, the boyfriends of the house standing discretely in the back; Vreeland and Carmel Snow, in hat and gloves, down in front with the other editors, maybe with Penn or Avedon beside them, and everybody watching the clients as the first models came out. I went to Dior, Givenchy, Chanel, Saint Laurent when he first opened his house, Madame Grès, and Balenciaga, who for me will always be the greatest designer. Going to his shows was an absolutely mouth-opening, awe-inspiring experience. Here was a man who wanted no publicity, craved none, except for his clothes. Once you've had a taste of celebrity—well, I won't say it destroys your talent, but, my God, the really great don't need it. The first time I ever saw corduroy used in couture was at Balenciaga. He made a typical Balenciaga suit—stand-away collar, three buttons—in plain old knockaround corduroy. That's when I started taking it up. And he had the most imaginative hats, without being Schiaparelli silly. And the coats: always made from the shoulder. Something else he did I thought was wonderful was to have a few models to whom the clients could relate. He liked rather plump Spanish models, with small protruding tummies and short limbs, but for a good ten years he actually had one who limped. Not that Balenciaga had so many disabled customers. But I think he felt there was something dignified about her, and she did look like a very rich lady, with a limp.

Don't think I wasn't dazzled by all this. I had my nose pressed right up to the glass, taking in everything. Two women I admired and saw often on those trips were Madame Clara and Hattie Carnegie. They, and Sophie Gimbel of Saks, ran the most successful custom salons in New York. All the great ladies of the Middle West, all the Pillsburies and Busches, all the women who were big, went to Madame Clara. She made them furs, too. And she made a fortune. I knew Hattie less well. Her shop was just off Madison, on 49th Street, and I loved going by to see the window displays. She always had just one garment in the window, suspended by wires and surrounded by the most beautiful hats and gloves and costume jewelry imaginable. But I don't think anyone really knew her. Carnegie wasn't even her real name. It was the name she picked up when she arrived at Ellis Island from Hungary. She said, "Who's the richest man in America?" Someone told her. And she said, "Okay, I'll be Hattie Carnegie." That should give you an idea of how she *saw* the world. She was married to a man who called himself Colonel. I doubt he was, but who cares? She would sit up all night playing bridge in an apartment that looked like Thelma Foy's, filled with French furniture, and the next day she'd be in her workroom barking at her designers: "We've got to have a basic little dress to walk the dogs!"*

But it was a rather small perspective. This is something that almost never comes across in fashion books and certainly not in magazines of that era—how truly small the fashion world was. Today fashion is digested globally, and seen globally, and understood globally. But in the fifties and early sixties, the fashion world was Mrs. Vreeland and Mrs. Snow sitting on gold salon chairs, smoking a lot.

You see, what Vreeland didn't understand about Norell was that he had pockets of devoted customers *all* over this country. We all did. And in places you'd never imagine. For instance, Norell had a mother-and-daughter team in the Midwest who bought only evening clothes. They couldn't get enough of them. He'd go to their home with a couple of trunks once or twice a year and

---

*Spared no doubt was Pauline Potter, Carnegie's designer before she became Pauline de Rothschild.

Stevie Kaufmann at Fire Island in the sixties.

they bought these thousand-dollar dresses as if they were nothing. They had hundreds of them. And the funny part of it was, they would only look at the clothes at night. Norell had to time his arrival for after the sun went down. He never did find out where their money came from or where they wore their dresses. But all of us had clients like that: rich and obscure as hell.

But, as a business, fashion had absolutely no social cachet in New York, the way banking or even advertising did. It wouldn't have held any interest for men like Gilbert Miller and Colonel Obolensky,* and I'm sure I wouldn't have held any interest for them if I hadn't learned to talk about something else. The people who worked on Seventh Avenue were considered trade. And the people themselves tended to foster this scorn. I remember Mollie Parnis telling my friend Stevie Kaufmann, before she realized who he was, "You go around the back door where you belong,"† when he came in through the front door on an errand for his family's

---

*Serge Obolensky, Russian aristocrat and well-known social figure in this period. The military rank is American; he served in the OSS during the war.

† Mollie, fortunately, was better known for the high-powered salons she ran in her Park Avenue apartment, and for dressing Mamie Eisenhower.

store. Paris always had a warm heart for the demimondaine aspects of fashion, because it saw designers as artists. But in New York, it wasn't until the sixties, when fashion was connected to the camp world of Pop artists and celebrity socialites—Baby Jane Holzer—that the establishment really accepted designers, and then with doubts. When I first started going out in the forties, to El Morocco and the 1-2-3 Club, I never saw any designers; models and assistants, sure. Occasionally I'd see Mainbocher at a private party, and Mainbocher dressed the grand dames as well as the young girls—C.Z., Kitty, Gloria Vanderbilt, and Princess Natasha Paley, who was his premiere *vendeuse* and was married to John C. Wilson, a theatrical agent, who, as Jack Wilson, had been Noël Coward's boyfriend. But Main himself tended to stay in the background, and I never saw him out publicly with the man he lived with, the illustrator Douglas Pollack.

Norell certainly never went out. He ate at Schrafft's every day. And always the same thing: scrambled eggs followed by vanilla ice cream with chocolate sauce. He had absolutely no interest in society, though he lived in the most beautiful duplex in Amster Yard. Exquisite pieces of furniture, not very much, on a highly polished mahogany floor. I loved his clothes—he was the first designer to make sequins legit outside the circus. But Norell himself had very little sparkle. Do you know, he never read a book unless someone gave him one? Although it figures that the last book he read before he died, in 1972, was Joan Blondell's *Center Door Fancy*. I say that because there are only two things that have ever influenced American fashion: Hollywood and society. Chanel may have taken her ideas from the playing fields of Eton, and Balenciaga from Goya and the Spanish infantas. But our royalty was Crawford and Brenda Frazier and whoever turned up in the flashbulbs Saturday night at the Stork Club.

As C.Z. alluded, I took over the design at Maurice Rentner and when Maurice died, in 1960, I got my name on the label, though it would be another decade before I could buy out the firm's owners, Eugene Lewin and Herman Seigenfeld. They were decent guys—no complaints. But they were typical manufacturers. They weren't eager to see me get recognition in my own right. This was something that no boss wanted for his designers, because it upset the status quo. But neither did they mind when my friendships with Adam Gimbel and Andrew Goodman, whom I saw out socially, brought the firm more business. And I can tell you, I be-

came a businessman inasmuch as I listened—to the salesmen who said, "We need more cocktail dresses for Dallas." There was no chichi. This was not Paris. On the other hand, Lewin and Seigenfeld and the others were too caught up in the old ways of doing business to recognize the importance of licensing a firm's name— something they vehemently opposed. And they couldn't see the budding new romance between socialites and designers, which, by the sixties, would be too hot for anyone not to notice.

In my mid-twenties, newly home from the war and not yet in civilian clothes, I had formed the idea of being a "presentable young man," a subtle tribute to glamour's lower entry requirements, and to the fact that, positionless and approaching insolvency, I had nothing whatsoever to present to the grown-up world. Still, funny things happened that I chalked up as progress. I remember having lunch with an army buddy, George Vandersluis, who later became a university professor, at a fashionable New York restaurant—don't ask me how we paid for this extravagance—and being invited to a picnic with the O'Connor sisters, Gloria and Consuelo,* then famous society models. Their mother had seen

---

*Later, Consuelo Crespi, wife of the Roman PR man Count Rudi Crespi.

us from across the room, asked us to join them for coffee, and I guess concluded from our uniforms and table manners that we were—well, presentable young men. But that's all it took in the sun-dappled, maypole-innocence of the late forties and fifties: a nice face and Mother's approval. I don't remember if George and I went to the picnic, but the fact that I have preserved this speck in amber should tell you how naïve and susceptible I was to glamour. I doubt the busy O'Connor sisters ever gave the moment another thought.

Going out at that time meant really only one thing: going to nightclubs. Residually, it meant getting drunk, and occasionally very drunk, and I am reminded that after one particularly drunken night I woke up to find myself wearing only my cuffs. Unable to extract the studs, I had cut my way out with a pair of nail scissors. There was no routine to these nighttime excursions, though I definitely had women under surveillance, and would often, the next morning, sketch a dress or an evening coat that had caught my eye. I would drop by any lounge where Bobby Short was playing, usually The Blue Angel. Or run over to The Monkey Bar to hear Bunny Pendleton. It was an era of great chanteuses— and clean hair and long, long necks. One night at El Morocco, I met a girl named Lucille Lang, who was Carnegie's fit model and would become mine at Anna Miller. Lucille lived for nightclubs. We would go out, often with another designer, Chuck Howard, who had come from Georgia and lived with the photographer George Platt-Lynes, and who was to give a young Donna Karan her start by introducing her to Anne Klein. Another fellow who was part of that era was Crawford Greenleaf. Crawford was a model, terrific-looking, with an aristocratic face—*and* funny. My God, we had great laughs together. About nothing. Much later, he married Ruth Lachman, whose first husband had been Charles Revson's partner, and, I believe, the source of the "L" in "Revlon." Ruth was funny. She was the only person I ever knew who would go to sleep snorkeling. She would just doze off. Had to be watched like a hawk.

CHUCK HOWARD: **I used to say to Bill, "I don't know how you do it, you're out every single night." But he was determined to be known, and he wasn't just out—he was out at the right parties. He just had this determination to be a star. The English accent I**

The Bill Blass Diet: Feel free

**would sometimes laugh at. But that's the way he wanted to
sound, so he did. And fortunately he had such a humor about it.**

I've often wondered: How *did* I afford to go to those clubs, where, in addition to cover charges, there were drinks to be bought and, of course, the requisite dinner jacket to be worn? Good question. I must have been taken a lot of places. But still . . . I was spending nearly every penny I made (about $250 per week in 1957) on clothes and shoes, thus earning, deservedly, the nickname Bootsie Blass. And I was traveling: to Spain for the bullfights with my friend Brindon Sherwood from Washington, to Cuba. I'll get to Cuba—and Fire Island—in a moment. That's what I've been leading up to, in a roundabout way.

Somehow, I did manage to have a nice apartment, on Madison near 63rd, and one day on the street I met Missy Weston. Missy was someone very much on the scene in the late fifties, though I didn't know her well. She was a model, but she was also society in that she had grown up in New York, at 555 Park Avenue, and Southampton, and was about to marry Tommy Bancroft, Elsie Woodward's grandson. Missy had a fabulous neck and head, and she was fun. Her parents were Minnie and Herbie Weston. Herbie always looked like a million bucks. People used to say he was the illegitimate son of the last kaiser, but I never thought the kaiser was handsome—and Herbie looked like a figure in an *Esquire* drawing. When he died, Missy gave me his 1924 Cartier watch. I still wear it. Minnie was Vreeland's closest friend in the world. They lived directly across Park from each other, and when Missy was a girl, they would wave to each other from their windows.

JOHN FAIRCHILD: **Missy and her husband, Tommy, were a
very attractive couple, and Missy was Bill's image of the
all-American chic girl—a younger version of C. Z. Guest.
Bill loved her and her family.**

Naturally Missy saw a lot of Diana growing up. I'll never forget the Thanksgiving dinner Missy had right after she and Tommy were married, and had moved to their new house on Long Island. We were nine around the table: Mrs. Woodward, her two grandsons, Billy Baldwin, Kitty Miller, Vreeland, and

Diana Vreeland outside her apartment.

myself. And, see, given an opportunity, Vreeland loved to take over the conversation. She would sit there and get into a position with her cigarette and then she would hold forth.

This was one of those days. Kitty, who was next to me, was visibly growing more agitated by Diana's performance. In her own houses, she was used to getting a crack in, but that day she couldn't get anything in.

Finally she turned to me and said, "You know, she's just *asking* for a knuckle sandwich." The line, delivered with startling movie-gangster relish—by a grand dame, about another grand dame—made me laugh. It still does.

I am struck by how things fell into place. Missy was to open a whole new world for me—Southampton, the Woodwards, Herbie and Minnie. And all from a single encounter on the street outside my apartment, when I had said: "Why don't you come up?" We talked five hours that day.

MISSY BANCROFT: **Bill was just this bright, warm, enthusiastic fellow. I remember the apartment was dark and very comfortable. It's intriguing how he's changed—how everything became starker**

and starker. He had these curtains in the apartment that were wonderful—and before anyone else had them. They were on a big pole and they were in heavy white cotton duck. They just stood out and they weren't lined.

But that's the way things happened in those days. Anything could happen, one felt, in an afternoon. One minute you were up in your office on Seventh Avenue, sketching a dress you had seen the night before at El Morocco, and the next . . . you were on the beach in Acapulco talking with Lana Turner and Johnny Stompanato. And don't forget what happened to him a few months later . . .

This is what I mean by experiencing things in brief incremental bursts. Nearly everything I've described, and am about to describe, took place in a matter of four or five years, between the end of the fifties and the beginning of the sixties. Then, except for the work and certain of the harder friendships, it would all be over for me. And another phase would begin.

Cuba: I have a photograph of myself and Brindon standing with the Cuban architect Evelio Piṇa at the bar, and I am most definitely swacked, in the drunken sense. Cuba was without a doubt the most wide-open, raucously glamorous society I have ever experienced. You went for sex and sun. Or, if you were rich, sex, sun, and the horse racing. I started going in 1954, and left on one of

1957.

the last planes, whenever it was that Castro came down from the hills with his guerrillas. I remember running into John Rawlings, the photographer, who was in Havana doing a shoot for *Vogue*, and the two of us casually discussing the danger. Christ, we were so oblivious. But Cuba had that effect on you. It made you not care what happened to you. I'd go down in January, right after the collections, usually with Stevie, or Chuck Howard, and we'd take rooms together at the Nationale Hotel.

> STEVEN KAUFMANN: **Bill was thin and blond, which he made blonder. He'd jump into the pool and it would come out purple . . . He'd go his way and I'd go mine. Every once in a while he'd stay out all night, and I'd be out looking for him. Now that I think about all this, he was the biggest slob. The example being that I came back to our suite one night. The lights were off. He was in bed. The drawers were out, the suitcases upside down, and I fell smack on my face. He was a big slob. Dropped everything.**

I don't think this is completely accurate. I just expected my stuff to be picked up.

Anyway, we'd be running around at night, as Stevie said. Havana had the most unbelievable whorehouses. There was a famous male bordello—I've forgotten the name. It was staggeringly pretty inside. The main room had a cathedral ceiling, and from the rafters swung an armada of model ships. You'd go in and the men would parade past. During the day we'd drive out to the beach or sit by the pool at the Nationale.

> STEVEN KAUFMANN: **There was a girl in Havana in those days—a Hungarian with a lot of pizzazz named Richter. Her family had a chemical factory in Cuba. She was madly in love with Bill. Of course, he gave her no time. To make it safe and sound with her, we invented a daughter for him. Called her Maria or Ann. Do you know that Richter sent me a Christmas card this year and in it she said, "How's my Old Daddy?" She lives in Rome.**

In the summers of this same period I was going to Fire Island. If the war and its experience had represented one kind of freedom, Fire Island was another. Plus this: It was just a terribly funny place. Even the boat ride over on Friday night was fun—the drunken parties. I don't remember many designers. I went out there first with Ray Dennis and John LaFarge, and we'd stay at Point of Woods, in the bachelor quarters there. Then we'd sneak out at night and go down to Cherry Grove, which was evil—well, it wasn't evil, but it was damn primitive. No electricity. It was something. A sexual paradise. That was the thing that made sex so exciting in those days: It was both open—*and* hidden. It was covered up; and yet at night, Cherry Grove—and, for that matter, Central Park—were chockablock.

For a couple of seasons I took a house with Tony Randall and his wife, Florence, who modeled for me, and another girl named Lila Degenstein. George Nardiello, another army buddy, whose father was the ring doctor at Madison Square Garden, would drop by. Joe Eula, who did the illustrations for Eugenia Sheppard in the *Herald Tribune*, had a place nearby. Later, around 1959, I rented a house with Glenn and Stevie. Among the occasional houseguests were Jerry Zipkin and Jacques Tiffeau, a rudely (and crudely) funny man who had been Dior's lover and was himself a talented designer. Jacques rarely missed an

*With Ruth Tankoos. She and her husband, Joe,
owned the Colony Hotel in Palm Beach.*

opportunity to insult or taunt someone—that summer it happened to be Zip,
who had an abhorrence of taking his clothes off on the beach. Jacques's problem
was that he couldn't keep his *on*, and was famous for stripping at parties—the
grander the better.

> JOE EULA: **None of us had any money then. Bill was well known,
> but we were all the bright young boys of the world. Halston
> wasn't anywhere near the scene. I don't think he had even
> arrived in New York yet. It was another world, because it
> really was not that sissy crap stuff. I mean, we were a gang.
> God, we laughed like crazy.**

Everybody always thinks they experienced a place best because they saw it first, but I think most of us knew we were on Fire Island at a time when it was truly special. Peggy Fears had just opened the Boatel in the Pines with her girl-friend Teddi Thurman. Peggy was a big-time chanteuse on Broadway, and was married to the producer A. C. Blumenthal, although she was with Teddi. Peggy was famous for singing a song that went, *"They say you only believe in"* . . . Sis Norris had a bar at Point of Woods, where Goldie Hawkins played the piano. Everybody went, gay or straight. You didn't know who was what; or you knew and didn't care. Those distinctions wouldn't be insisted on for another decade.

I wouldn't have missed Fire Island. It was so much a part of one's grow-ing up. But just as I knew I didn't want to be part of the "cloakies," I also didn't want to be one of the boys. So I stopped going to Fire Island after 1961.

Then one day that summer I was sitting on the beach with Louise. We used to feel a bit competitive, Louise and I, perhaps because we hit the scene at the same time. Her mother, Ruth Tankoos, positively worshiped her. Ah, spoiled! We've been friends, always.

With Michael Pardo, the son of model Pat Ryan.

So we were sitting there and we saw this figure coming down the beach toward us with crimped black hair and wearing an eye-catching caftan, a big straw hat, and many scarves.

Louise started to laugh. "Oh, my God, it's Betsy *Pickering*!"*

"Don't be an ass," I said, "it's Kenny Lane."

KENNETH JAY LANE: **Bill's humor is not after someone else's. I remember going with him to Peru. It was Christmastime. We got off the plane and there were some reporters—I guess, because there had been some publicity in the Lima paper. The headline said something like: "The dressmaker and jeweler of Jackie Kennedy are in town." What! Later, someone asked Bill where he was from and he said, "Indiana." The person said, "Oh, where's that?" And Bill said, "Outside of London."**

---

*A.k.a., Betsy Theodoracopulos, a model of that era, now Betsy Kaiser.

5

M e n

I've always preferred men who are men. Gable, to me, was the sexiest man alive. Gable couldn't do anything that wasn't one hundred percent masculine. Everyone knows what Crawford meant when she said that being next to him gave her "twinges of a sexual urge beyond belief"—and Crawford was only referring to their *on*-screen chemistry. But unless you saw him playing a cheap vaudeville hoofer in *Idiot's Delight*, you might never know that his confidence wasn't limited to a manly growl. It ran all the way to his toes. Men of that era didn't just frisk you politely with their sexuality. They stunned you with it. Years ago, at the Ivy in London, I remember the room suddenly going dead quiet. Olivier was there that day. Coward. Everybody in the world. I looked up and there was this great big guy standing at the entrance. I said to the fellow I was with, "Who in the world is *that?*" Everybody had their eyes on this man in the door. My friend said, "He's a new actor who's going to make the first Bond movie. His name is Sean Connery." He was, without question, in the flesh—six-foot-three, whatever—the most magnetic man.

There will always be people for whom a room will go silent, but I don't think I'm expressing the opinion strictly of my generation when I say that the leading men of today, a Cruise or a Clooney, don't have the same effect. I am not speaking of their sexuality—I wouldn't know or care about that—but only of their masculinity. There is something not one hundred percent about it. Imagine how insignificant their wattage would seem in a room if Gable suddenly walked in? One has the sense, too, that they have been "styled," or given style; but, in any case, have not taken the trouble to find style themselves. It is cardboard style. There's nothing you can get off it, learn.

People forget how much movie stars taught us about dressing—and none more so than Gary Cooper.* Every man wanted to look like Cooper, just as practically every gal on the Upper East Side of New York wanted to look like Babe Paley. I was in Paris a few years after Bacall married Bogart, and Rocky Cooper was a friend of mine. One afternoon I saw the four of them lunching together. With her immaculately fresh hair, and wearing something incredibly sleek, Bacall certainly stood out from all the French women. But it was Cooper who really stood out. Believe me, he was the best-looking son of a bitch who ever lived. He had the greatest sense of style. Do you remember that scene in *Love in the Afternoon*—it's rather late in the action—when he leaves the Ritz with the collar of his coat turned up and his shirttails flapping? Up until then his character has been the picture of savoir faire, but now he's completely undone by this anonymous French girl (Audrey Hepburn). I'm sure it was Cooper's idea to leave the tails out. He wouldn't have needed a director to tell him how sexy that gesture was. You see, it was no accident that Cooper looked as terrific as he did. A few years ago, while writing an article for *Esquire* about Cooper's style, I had a couple of long chats with Rocky and their daughter Maria. It was fascinating. They told me he used to go on these shopping expeditions in Rome and Paris. He'd buy cottons by the yard in Mexico and then send them to a shirtmaker in Italy. He had tailors all over the world, and he was the first to buy jeans and do the stone-washed thing. He'd beat them on a rock and leave them out in the sun all day. Did it himself, too.

There have been only a few men in my life with whom I have felt very close. Certainly Ed Guild was one, and I am aware that some of my later friendships— with Tim Healy, for instance, the Jesuit priest who was head of the New York Pub-

*Though now much maligned and overreferenced, the Duke of Windsor exerted more fashion influence than any man of the twentieth century. Not only was he responsible for getting millions of men into pleated trousers, he also had the imagination to ask his tailor, H. Harris on East 59th Street, to insert a removable cotton lining in his golfing trousers so he wouldn't have the bother of wearing underpants. This was not one of the details he shared with me when we met at a dinner party in the fifties at Eleanor Lambert's, though I was surprised at his willingness to talk at length about his clothes. And he is still, for me, the only man of relatively small size who could mix different plaids without looking like a racing tout.

lic Library for an all-too-brief period in the late eighties and early nineties—were attempts to experience that same quality of trust and companionship, when you can tell the other person anything you want, and there is no sense of rivalry. Niki de Gunzburg was someone who was important to me. I can only tell you I found his company very stimulating. Joe Eula once did a wonderful sketch of the two of us standing at the bar at the Ritz. Not much larger than a postcard, it is one of the few pictures or drawings of a personal nature that I keep out—on a desk as you come into my house in Connecticut. But Niki had a reticence about his sexuality—really, a reticence about anything connected to his private life—that kept even his friends at a slight distance. Maybe that's why I liked him. You couldn't pin Niki down.

I've had one or two love affairs in my life. I'm eighty years old for God's sake—don't you imagine *something* might have happened? But considering that I've never lived with another person, I don't think it would be an exaggeration to say that I have a problem with confinement. I was going to say commitment, but as I reflect on my tendency not to stay in a situation or place too long, be-ginning with Indiana, I think the other term better describes my feelings. Of course, the war represented a period of intense physical confinement, but we all knew that situation couldn't last forever.

No, what I am referring to is something more general—and specific.

Although I have never made any attempt to conceal my sexuality, neither have I ever wanted to flaunt it. Moreover, to have lived in a long-term relation-ship with a man would have been to categorize myself too narrowly. Because, in so many cases, I've been attracted to women. To the romance part plus the ac-ceptance of a hetero relationship—that being the most natural way, in my opin-ion, to live one's life. But I never wanted marriage to a woman any more than I wanted an openly gay relationship with a man. It was a question of conduct—conduct, perhaps, being the last refuge of a coward—but also I knew I could be easily dominated by a partner, though maybe not a woman. This was the wall I eventually hit in my friendship with Slim Keith. She wanted a more formal arrangement—marriage—and I didn't. So that was the end of us being friends. But I don't see how such a marriage can ever be fair. It's not fair because the only one truly benefiting is the male—and then she's responsible for taking care of you when you turn out to be an old prick anyway.

JOHN RICHARDSON: **Before he was ill, and I think things have changed now, there was an imaginary line around Bill, and you crossed it at your own peril. If you knew Bill and loved Bill, you knew your friendship to some extent depended on not ever crossing this line. What is difficult with Bill is that he's so cordial and affectionate that if you're not aware of the line and cross it, things suddenly will go cool. And Slim, who was such a wise old bird, for some reason didn't know this. I think she was just besotted.**

But nowhere did I feel more confined than on Seventh Avenue. As my career was the only thing that mattered to me, it wasn't enough that I had crossed divides in other areas of my life. The challenge was to do it in a business as insular as fashion, where, according to the rigid mentality of the manufacturers, a designer couldn't even have a couple of evening dresses in a collection if the label was known for suits. Though Lewin and Seigenfeld were opposed to my getting recognition, it ceased to be an issue once we started to advertise, in the early sixties, with tag lines like "Positively Blassfamous" and "They can't knock off Bill Blass." Jane Trahey was the brain behind the ads, and I still think they sparkle with unexpected wit. In one, I am having a heart-to-heart with Dr. Joyce Brothers. In another, from 1966, which played against type as well as on snob appeal, a photograph of a dashing businessman appeared above the caption:

> *How Do You Compete with a Husband Like This?*
> *Screen the galleries on 57th Street for him.*
> *Study the complexities of his Maserati.*
> *Learn to sail before the Larchmont Regatta.*
> *Discriminate between Louis XIV and XV.*
> *Speak a third language (American and French are not enough).*
> *Hire a fencing master.*
> *Angel a hit play (anyone can angel a loser).*
> *Try out-dressing him—make Bill Blass your designer.*

Not alert to the power of name recognition, Lewin and Seigenfeld were even less alive to the idea of my getting into licensing, which was just starting to take off. The first licenses I did were children's clothes and a line of swimsuits, for Roxanne. One suit I especially remember was strapless, with an Empire waist and a skirt of white reembroidered lace. Not exactly practical for the beach, but that wasn't the point. We got a lot of attention from that suit. But being old school, Lewin and Seigenfeld figured they were making enough money with the Rentner name alone. Why screw it up? But the world of women's fashion is really too small to (a) make any money, and (b) exert an influence in a country as big as this one. I remember the Hanes men's underwear people did a survey once in which they asked guys in bars and factories and so forth what my name meant to them, if anything, and they said, "Oh, he's the fellow who does the car." At that point, I'd been in fashion thirty years, had won the Coty Award three or four times, and had been in most of the magazines. Yet they knew me from an automobile I had little to do with except recommend color schemes, and, as we know, couldn't drive.

The two things that really put my name over were going on the road to other cities and doing men's wear. Obviously, at the time, I was too involved to understand what this meant, but I realize now that both pursuits were a reaction to the smallness and effeminacy of the fashion world—just as my war experience had represented another kind of break from the singularity of fashion. It wasn't

The Blass edition of the Lincoln Continental.

that I hated the fag elements of fashion; it was that I hated the limits that fashion imposed. And the way I chose to set myself apart, consciously or unconsciously, was through the world of men.

MICA ERTEGUN: **There's nothing feminine about that apartment on Sutton Place or the Connecticut house. There's nothing feminine about the way he entertains. The flowers are not feminine. There's just a bunch of one kind. You see, I never thought of Bill as being homosexual, compared to someone who might have a double life. He never struck me as that. Everything about Bill, his gestures, his taste, is masculine.**

I threw myself into designing the first men's collections. It was David Pincus, of Pincus Brothers Maxwell, a men's manufacturer in Philadelphia, who came to me with the idea, in 1967, though I don't think we would have gone anywhere without Mildred Custin, who had just taken over Bonwit's. Mildred was one of the first retailers to see that, in order to sell a tie or a shirt, you needed an overall look. Plus the excitement of a personalized boutique. One day she asked me what I was doing and I told about the men's line, and she said, "I want it. Sight unseen." And she wanted to open the boutique with a party, at night, with klieg lights—unheard of in those days.* Poor Adam Gimbel didn't get it. He couldn't understand opening a store at night for a party.

So I started going to Italy for shoes and leather goods. Have you ever been to Parma? My God, the food in Parma. Anyway, in the beginning, we had our suits made in Italy, from English fabric. I'd go to the mills in Huddersfield, England, where they keep records back to the eighteenth century, and I'd find patterns worn by the Duke of Windsor. In his lifetime, if he ordered a pattern, it couldn't be sold to anyone else. He had a heather-blue suit with white window-

---

*Mildred was, in fact, already selling Pierre Cardin's men's clothes, having been sold on the idea by the publicist Eleanor Lambert. The daughter of a circus advance man from Crawfordsville, Indiana, Eleanor helped many fashion careers, including mine. And, of course, she presides over the International Best-Dressed List. She did so much just in the way of forwarding American fashion. And it didn't hurt anyone who knew Eleanor that she and her late husband, Seymour Berkson, publisher of the *New York Journal-American*, were prominent socially, too.

pane checks that was terrific. I bought bolts of that, and it became a success. I did a kilt, too, which I showed on a big, halfback-looking guy—couldn't have been straighter—named Ken Albrecht. Another look I liked a lot from that period was a coat based on a World War I trench coat. I still have it in my archives.

In the fifties, I had my clothes made by Lord, which was an offshoot of another custom place called Chipp (both long gone). There, I would experiment. I'd say to the tailor, "Let's do a blazer for summer in brown linen, instead of navy blue." I thought a brown one would look good with white pants. In those days, there was a writer for *Esquire* named George Frazier—a terrific snob, rather like the society columnist Lucius Beebe—who compiled the magazine's best-dressed list. He heard about me from Lord and one day phoned me up. He asked about my clothes. Then he said, "And your club?" I said, "Hey, I belong to Diner's Club!" There was a long pause and then he roared. He did list me, but when I came out with my men's collection, he took a terrible swipe at me. He said the clothes were vulgar.

Actually, what I was shooting for was swagger—a cross between Damon Runyan and the Duke of Windsor, or what the fashion editor Sally Kirkland, after seeing my first show, called "the Scarsdale Mafia look." I loved the expressive masculine style of the thirties. I didn't give a damn about tastefulness. A few years later, Ralph Lauren was to build his empire around WASP tastefulness, and today, in my opinion, his is the only American fashion brand that has truly succeeded on a global scale. Ralph had realized, while he was still in the tie business, that if he didn't want to make what looked like garmento ties, he had to go the other way—make Brooks Brothers look a little more English-club-looking. I, on the other hand, was only interested in satisfying my own tastes. I probably sensed I was out on a limb with my men's clothes, but, just the same, I enjoyed the risks.

The person who influenced me more than anyone, of course, was Niki. It seems unbelievable that someone who, as I say, always wore the same type of dark suit and white shirt could influence anyone except a Bible salesman. And though one can point to any number of contemporary designers who have taken up that style (Hedi Slimane of Dior is the most obvious), I suppose in some ways Niki was a slave to it. Once, in the seventies, I took a house in Jamaica and Niki came to stay for a week. Afterward, I suggested he join me in Palm Beach, where

They can't knock off Bill Blass.

Seventh Avenue gets away with murder. Somebody creates a hot design and bang, before he even gets it in the stores they knock it off. That's why Bill Blass got himself some protection. The protection of exclusive fabrics nobody else can have. Of subtle nuances of cut, of shaping and of draping. Of thousands of details so tiny nobody but Blass even knows they're there. Next time you want something knockout that won't be knocked off, get yourself some protection. Invest in Bill Blass.

I had business. He hadn't been in Palm Beach in twenty years, not since Mona Williams had a house there.

Well, Niki arrived but his luggage didn't. He was in a state. "What am I going to do? You don't understand. I've never even had a ready-made tie." Not having a tie in Palm Beach, much less a custom tie, would only be a problem for someone whose idea of summer clothes was the same black pants and white shirt he wore in the winter. But Niki knew exactly what he wanted, and it was his sense of discipline and order—a sense he had in common with Billy Baldwin— that influenced me. And it applied to rooms as well as fashion. I went through a period of having a lot of clutter around, and Niki told me something that has always stayed in my mind. He had a knack for the crisp observation, too. He said, "Clutter only works, my dear, when it's the value of Chanel's."

Later in his life—I guess, after he had stopped looking for his inheritance—Niki bought a small chalet on an island in a lake in New Jersey. He lived there with a man named Paul Sherman, an artist, and Niki made the place absolutely charming. He had these heavy winter curtains made of loden cloth piped in brown leather. I only went there in winter so we could ice skate. Because I do ice skate. I was bad. He was really good.

GRACE MIRABELLA: **Niki and Bill shared the world of Cole Porter and Noël Coward, the musical stage, that world and that moment, and it was often reflected in Blass's clothes. I remember a wonderful photograph that John Rawlings took, a still-life of the contents of a man's pocket that had been emptied and thrown on the floor. The brand of cigarette at that time, the knife, a little money—but marvelous things. And in the picture, you saw the end of a pair of men's trousers— the ankles, the black silk socks, and a perfect black shoe. I said, "God, everything about this picture is perfect." And Niki replied, "Of course, dear, it's mine."**

We showed the first men's collections on the promenade at Avery Fisher Hall. We set up the runway between the two escalators, and the guys would go

Paul Sherman and myself ice skating at Niki's.
I have a couple of portraits Paul did of me somewhere in the attic.

up one and come down the other. In those days, I used to do a little running commentary as the models were coming out. I'd say, "Here is Ken in a . . ." and so forth. Everyone came to those shows, men and women, and Ralph later told me he loved seeing them. Usually we had a theme. One season I did a collection around Gatsby, with flashy plaid and white suits. Another time it was the Alain Delon movie *Borsolino*. For that show, I had the first six guys come out in double-breasted striped suits, with violin cases and, of course, Borsolino hats. They looked terrific. But then, this was the era when all the models looked good. Buck Class: He was better looking than Delon himself. Bill Loock. Loock, who only stopped modeling a few years ago, at seventy-five, raised four children with his wife, though he didn't for one minute look like a realistic father. If you saw him today coming up the walk, you'd say, "Wow."

BILL LOOCK: **I started traveling around the country with Bill, doing shows for charities. San Francisco, La Jolla, Chicago. We smoked enough cigarettes and drank enough martinis to sink a ship.**

One day in the middle of all that barnstorming I got a call from Cary Grant, kindly inviting me to share his private plane for a few cities. Cary was then making promotional appearances on behalf of the fragrance company Fabergé. For Cary, this largely entailed flying to a city, answering questions at a press conference that would be convened at his hotel, and essentially being Cary Grant. He didn't actually promote any products in a store. We flew out to Dayton, Ohio, where I was doing a show for Rike's department store, and agreed to meet later for a drink. Midway through my stand-up routine at the podium, as the models were strolling out, the audience gave a slight gasp. I turned around, and there was Cary. He had slipped in through the back. Well, the audience went wild. He took the microphone and said quite a few words before the show resumed. Later I said to him, "Why the hell couldn't you have done that in New York?"

When I won the first Coty Award given for men's wear, in 1968, David Pincus, who had been a discus thrower in college, suggested I ask athletes to model for the awards presentation at the Metropolitan Museum. We had several

At Lincoln Center with Niki de Gunzburg (center) and Jacques Tiffeau.

that night, including the tennis champion Tony Trabert and Jessie Owens, the first black athlete to win multiple Olympic gold medals, and whose victory in track at the 1936 games in Berlin had meant so much to people in this country.

The success of the first collections was immediate. Men were going into Bonwit's and buying shoes without even trying them on. There was no place to sit down anyway. They would hold up the shoes to the bottom of their feet, and say, "That's a fit. I'll take them." The custom at that time was for men and women to go to lunch on Saturdays and then shop together. They'd hit Bloomingdale's, Bonwit's, all the boutiques and art galleries on Madison—the socializing parade that Tom Wolfe described in his essay "The Saturday Route." One day I was in my boutique in Bonwit's and I saw this black lady in her cloth coat and worn shoes. She looked like somebody's cook. Not a salesman would wait on her. All these grand fags, and they were all fussing over whatever celebrities were there.

So I went over to the lady and I said, "Miss Fitzgerald, can I help you?"

She said, "Yeah, I'm closing tonight at the Waldorf and I want twenty-six blazers, twenty-six pairs of pants, twenty-six shirts, and twenty-six ties. Do you think you can get someone to help me?"

I said, "I think I can," and I went over to one of the salesmen. I said, "Get your ass over there, you son of a bitch. That's Ella Fitzgerald and she'll give you the biggest order you've had all week." She wanted the clothes as gifts for the guys in her orchestra, but nobody knew who she was. I remember Stanley Marcus telling me years ago, when I first started selling at Neiman's, that they never disregarded the homesteader and his wife who came into the store in their country clothes. You never knew who was going to hit oil that day. And as Stanley said, "If you took care of them, they and their children and their grandchildren would be customers for life."

Because of the popularity of my men's wear, Charles Revson wanted to license my name to a men's fragrance. He wasn't interested in doing a woman's perfume for me, because he had launched Norell and was having such a success with it. He only wanted the men's thing. I had no experience with a big-time license—though I doubt anyone could have dealt with Charles and come out ahead.

I liked Charles, in the short span that I knew him. He invited me to his parties and, socially, he and his wife, Lyn, were nice. They had a huge apartment, a triplex that now belongs to Henry Kravis, and his yacht, the *Ultima II*, was the biggest thing going. Their parties were unique. Charles would have five-kilo cans of caviar all over the place, on every table. He did something else that I had never seen, at least at the time. When the first course had been served, which was probably caviar again—this time with a baked potato, which was just coming into vogue—the butler would say, "What would you like for the next course? Will you have meat, fish, or chicken?" The butler had been Winston Churchill's butler at Chequers, and they called him Mister Thorpe, or whatever his name was. They didn't call him Thorpe. They called him Mister Thorpe.

After dinner, bingo would be played. The butler would stand at the front of the room and call out the letters. The prizes were always fabulous. A pair of gold Cartier cuff links. Matching sets of Gucci or Hermès luggage. A toilet seat embedded with dollar bills. Lavish gifts—and fun, too. I was there one night with Oscar and Françoise de la Renta, and Oscar showed me how you could more easily win by taking two cards, though, honestly, I couldn't keep one going and I never won a thing.

But Charles was not a man of humor. Was he not! He was crazy about having all the related fragrance products—the bronzer, the deodorant, the soap, the after-shave, the conditioners. We had about twenty products. Then he came out with something called Men's Other Deodorant—for the crotch. I was amused.

I said, "You mean to tell me a man will use a different deodorant than the one he puts under his arms?"

Charles said, "Just wait. You'll see."

So we launched it, in a subtle way. You can't say "crotch." You say "other." Anyway, one day I got a letter in my office from a gentleman in Baton Rouge, Louisiana, who wrote: "Mr. Blass, I love your new men's product called Other, but I have one problem that I think I ought to bring to your attention. And that is every time I use it, I get an erection."

I thought: Oh, my God, we'll make a fortune. I called Charles. And, you know, to get hold of Charles Revson on the phone—it would be easier to reach the White House. He had half a dozen secretaries. I persisted, "No, I've got to talk to Mr. Revson personally. It's very important." He finally took the call and I said, "Charles, we're about to make a fortune." He growled, "What are you talking about?" I read him the letter.

A pause, and then: "That's not funny!" He banged down the phone and never mentioned it again.

As I say, Charles had a lot of assistants and secretaries. He came in after lunch and worked until nine or ten at night, and he expected his people to be at their posts from nine in the morning. He was constantly firing people, and one day he fired this guy. The man hung around the office until the end of the day, and then he asked one of the secretaries if he could see Mr. Revson before he left. He was shown in and he said, "Mr. Revson, you can't fire me." Charles growled, "Why not?" The guy said, "Because I'm madly in love with you!"

With that, Charles started buzzing every buzzer on his desk. He had buttons for all over the world—London, Paris. Everyone came running.

Get him out of here!

Years after the initial big splash of the men's fragrance, when it had almost faded from sight, I ran into Franco Zeffirelli in Rome and he said, "I'm crazy about your men's fragrance." I said, "How in the world . . ." He explained to me that a friend of his stocked it in his perfume shop. I doubt Charles made much money on it, though. I know I never made any money with him, period.

The scent was so erotic for that time. I still have a tiny bit in a bottle in New York.

In the end, the men's wear collections could not sustain their original level of design and custom workmanship. The garment unions threatened to shut Pincus down if he continued to use Italian factories, and once the stores had access to our sources in Italy, they could go to them directly for their own sweaters and shoes. My interest diminished when things could not be made at a high quality, and by 1970, when I bought out Lewin and Seigenfeld, I had too many other concerns to concentrate solely on winning that battle. Which has become almost an unwinnable battle in an era that spends an extraordinary amount on clothes, yet places little value on the telling gestures of style. And strange as it must sound, I think people are still desperate to learn.

But the men's collections, in addition to serving as the test case for Ralph and Perry Ellis, did mark a kind of beginning for me. They established my name outside the small world of women's fashion, and it was because of my men's clothes that so many women came to me and said, "Won't you make a raincoat or a checked suit like our husbands' for us?" That was how I started my second women's line, Blassport.

6

W o m e n

I really wasn't prepared when Bette Davis turned me down, although I see now
how this hardheaded, truthful Yankee—once dismissed by Carl Laemmle Jr. of
Universal Studios as "a cotton-dress girl"*—might have thought she was being
given special treatment when I invited her to come in and buy some clothes. She
is the only woman I ever knew who felt pinched, morally, by a bargain. And,
honestly, it was no bargain. The truth is movie stars were always coming to Seventh Avenue, or to the smaller custom salons like Mainbocher or Hattie
Carnegie, to order clothes, and they paid for them, with hard currency—not the
quid pro quo of publicity. Adrian and Norell, who between them dressed Joan
Crawford, Norma Shearer, and Loretta Young, treated their Hollywood clients
like royalty, but sent them a bill just the same, and certainly mere mortals had
a chance to buy wholesale, on Saturdays, when Seventh Avenue opened its doors
to anyone who could claim an "uncle" in the business. Indeed, the Saturday
openings were good for business. They were a thrifty way to unload deadbeat in-
ventory. Nowadays, the frank pursuit of celebrities by designers has degenerated
into a glorified swap meet—your publicity for my free dress. It is commerce of
another kind, and it's too far gone to bother condemning. But wouldn't it be

*And the title of Janet Flanner's splendid 1943 profile of Davis in *The New Yorker*.

good for the soul of a designer if the next time he offered clothes to an actress—
or even, more ecumenically, the invitation to buy them at wholesale—she firmly
rapped his knuckles like an old-fashioned schoolmarm?

One afternoon Miss Davis telephoned me at the office.

"This is Bette Davis," she announced. Her voice, at once familiar and
spine-tingling, made me sit up straighter.

"Yes, Miss Davis?"

"I'm in Dallas, at Neiman's, and I've just bought some of your clothes
and I've never seen anything so divine." She carried on like this for a few deliri-
ous moments.

When it was my turn to speak, I said, "That's so kind of you, Miss Davis.
If you like the clothes, why don't you come here the next time you're in New York
and get some things."

There followed a disconcerting pause. "I should say not!" she shot back.
"I don't believe in this thing of people going to one's place of manufacturing and
buying clothes. You're in business for the same reason that Neiman Marcus is,
and that's where it should end."

Unfortunately that's where my relations with Miss Davis ended as well. I
would have gladly sent anything she desired to the nearest Neiman's branch, if
it would have satisfied her New England principles. But no matter. I have always
treasured our conversation. It gave me a glimpse into what made this lustrous
pain in the neck a box-office star, and, for my money, her prim slap was just
plain gutsy.

I've never dressed anyone solely for publicity value—the Versace syndrome. Saint Laurent never went out of his way to dress celebrities, either; and
I don't put Deneuve in that category, because after she entered his world, in 1968
or something, he seemed satisfied with his share of the heavens, and closed the
hatch. One goddess was enough. Givenchy had his collaboration with Audrey
Hepburn, but in a way it presented a problem for him. Because when she said,
"His are the only clothes in which I am myself," did that mean Givenchy was
only at his best when he dressed Audrey? This is something that designers with
many kinds of clients, many facets to their business, have to think about if they
hope to Be Around to dress anybody.

CHESSY RAYNER: **Bill really got on the bandwagon early in getting certain women to wear his clothes. I'm not saying he went after them, but if they came to him, he opened the door. Not just a crack, but all the way. So he really got everyone in town wearing those dresses. The effect was that people out in the sticks were dying to wear them, too.***

Naturally, I offered women wholesale, in or out of Hollywood. I loved the times when Paulette Goddard would drop by. She was a great friend of Warhol's, and often would be on her way downtown to see him. We would sit and bitch for hours. How old was Paulette then? She wasn't young. I had a black pailletted suit with silver fox cuffs that I called my Linda Porter suit. Niki photographed it in *Vogue*. Paulette ordered the suit in white, with white fox. It sounds vulgar but it wasn't. All those years of standing in front of a camera had been better than a mirror for Paulette. Another whose visits I looked forward to was Raquel Welch. Raquel, needless to say, had a terrific body, and that great mane, and as she was then at the peak of her fame, her arrivals caused a mild stir in the lobby at 550 Seventh Avenue. But she couldn't have been funnier or more down-to-earth; and despite her tendency to wear costumes of astonishing smallness, she appreciated well-made clothes.

I never could take the hair under the arms, though, of that other girl—Faye Dunaway. Do you remember that famous picture of her with her arms up? As gestures go, that one wouldn't be my idea of authentic. The hair—God, yes. It wasn't Dynel. But the gesture: I averted my gaze.

In the past, I have stated somewhat glibly, but not inaccurately, that much of my early success as a designer arose from the fact that women saw me as an extra man with a dinner jacket. I supplied a nice balance to their boy-girl-boy-girl *placement*. And don't forget that in those days, in the late forties and fifties, women had different expectations of men. I don't mean the standards were lower, but certainly they were not as highly evolved as they are today. Women, then,

*From an unpublished interview Chessy gave in 1996, two years before her death.

liked a man who smoked, enjoyed the odd drink, and could dance without crushing their hair. Knowing the words to popular songs helped, too. It was just a much simpler time. And I am reminded of how simple my outlook was, too, by an ad I ran in the seventies for my perfume. Under the heading "What I like and don't like so much in a woman," I listed ten things. Here are the top five:

My dislikes	My likes
1. A woman who talks about dieting all the time.	*1. A woman who seems to be listening, even if she isn't.*
2. Who does crossword puzzles in ink.	*2. A woman who loves a good laugh.*
3. A woman who jogs and tells.	*3. Who can get gorgeously dressed in 15 minutes flat.*
4. A woman whose perfume is too loud for her looks.	*4. Who can cuss in five languages.*
5. A woman who can't pass a mirror without looking into it.	*5. Who prefers almost anything to white wine.*

I have, of course, described an ideal: the man's woman. And I can't remember a time when this wasn't my ideal. But I can see now—or, rather, I can say now—that what made this ideal work for me, far more than the dinner jacket or any of that, was the way I talked to women. I talked to them straight—no crapola. It's a little like talking to a man. Because although a woman can handle almost anything you throw at her, a man, almost out of sheer laziness, will act as if he has nothing riding on the outcome of a situation. He doesn't get needlessly carried away with concern. He is involved, because he feels a sense of responsibility to his family or his business; yet, at the same time, he does a wonderful impersonation of a man going over the falls in a barrel: "What, me, worry?" I think women find this vaguely disinterested attitude very reassuring, especially in fashion, where people are prone to either exaggerate or worry everything to death. I remember when Casey and Abe Ribicoff were buying their apartment in my building, on Sutton Place, and, naturally, they were eager to make a good impression before the co-op board and its president, the decorator

*On Fifth Avenue with Louise.
She gave me the Frenchy
nickname Guy, while I
called her—still do—Luigi.*

Betty Sherrill. Nothing turns a solid New Yorker into a puree of nerves like the thought of being rejected by a co-op board. But it is precisely at such times that one shouldn't overthink a damn thing. So when Casey asked me how she should proceed, I said, "Just shut up, and wear a WASPy bow in your hair."

LYNN WYATT: **I remember the first thing he said to me. I had on this stunning bronze and brown satin dress with a low neck. I could wear it today, and this was twenty-five years ago. He came up to me and said, "Oh." Of course, he knew the dress was his. I said, "What? You don't like it?" And he said, "Yes, but you have it on backward." I told him I wanted the low part in the back. And he said, "Well, it looks great, babe."**

Perhaps because I tend to avoid all forms of entanglement myself, I try to keep my advice simple, topping it off with humor. Of course, you can't say to a woman stepping out of a fitting room, her face beaming with hope, "Oh, my God, that makes you look fat." But you can say, "Kid, that's not you. Let's try something else." She can accept that without embarrassment, and the fitting chugs along. Among the women I dressed, or who merely dropped by for a cigarette and a chat, I made no deference to age or social rank. I spoke the same way to Brooke Astor and Judy Peabody's mother, Mrs. Dennington, a very formidable lady, as I did to the younger gals like Pat Buckley and Nina Griscom.

> JUDY PEABODY: **My mother used to fidget a lot and would fuss with her hair or something. And Bill would say, "Liz, stop that." She behaved because it was him. Once, during a fitting for a suit, she kept raising her arms, and Bill said, "Take your hands off that collar." She said, "But it's going up on the sides." And he said, "That's my job, not yours. Now stand still." Nobody talked to my mother like that. But he did. Bill could boss his ladies around.**

Before I sold my business and retired, in 1999, I arrived at the office at eight in the morning. We were always busy. In the eighties, I had a secretary named Sue Blair, who a couple of decades earlier, during her marriage to a *New York Times* correspondent, had met the Fairchilds in Paris and been something of a muse to the designer François Crahay of Nina Ricci. So Sue was a bit more than a secretary. Harold Davis, who ran the sales department, used to complain that the place was like a country club. Not that it looked anything like a country club, but the atmosphere was very relaxed and all sorts of people were coming in. Nancy Kissinger often came by with Tyler, her yellow Lab, and he'd stretch out under my desk while Nancy and I caught up.

Nancy Kissinger in 1977, with her Lab, Tyler, under my desk.

My office in those days was rather large, with beige carpeting and white walls, and bookshelves on either side as you walked in. I had a few good photographs, including Horst's portrait of Dietrich and another by an unknown photographer of Cooper, as well as Eric's drawing of Chanel and one he did of a leopard halter I made to go with a cream chiffon skirt. Chessy's mother, Chesborough Armory Patvévitch, whom everyone called Big Chessy, ordered that outfit. There was a small sofa and a few chairs for guests. I worked at a large, off-white marble table in front of a pair of windows. Beyond them was a narrow terrace for shrubbery, and beyond that, twelve floors down, was Seventh Avenue. When I left the business, the carpet was stained with burn marks—from the girls smoking.

> MICA ERTEGUN: **When you went up to see Bill, it was fun. It wasn't like going and trying on a dress. He was always pulling things out and saying, "This would be very chic to wear." I remember he had some satin blouses and he gave me a black one and a white one, and he said, "Wear one on top of the other." And I'll tell you, it was the chicest thing.**

Chessy was the first to start coming in. That was in 1953, when she was a junior editor at *Ladies' Home Journal* and I was taking my first tentative steps out of the backroom at Anna Miller. She moved along to *Glamour* and *Vogue*, and we became friends. Chessy had a wonderful sense of style, although it is only in our time that we could have appreciated someone with her distinctive look, and equated it with beauty. Her mother was a beauty from forever, and I think that must have been a source of frustration for Chessy growing up. It is for so many women. There was something tragic about Chessy. There were secrets I have no idea about, though I'm sure they had to do with those ritual childhood warnings about ugly ducklings. But this is only a guess. I remember going to Chessy's funeral and catching Annette de la Renta's eye, in a way that a friend will, just as Big Chessy entered the church, perfectly turned out in black. All I can tell you is that the best-looking woman in the church was Chessy's mother.

*With
Chessy Rayner.*

ANNETTE DE LA RENTA: **Bill was incredibly kind to Chessy, and loving—and you know he hates to be loving, so he would never admit that. But he was. Bill understood it all—her, her look, how American she was.**

I've known many women who had great taste and a flair for dressing, but only two whose style unquestionably was their own. One was Chessy and the other was Slim Keith. Chessy was the first in her crowd to mix and match, to use color in imaginative ways, and to put on something as austere as a gray flannel skirt with a white blouse and make it look chic. She dressed so simply. With her skinny body and smooth cap of hair, she could wear Madame Grès's couture drapes as well as a boy's T-shirt and a pair of khakis. In fact, before anyone else picked up on it, she was buying things at the army-navy store on 42nd Street, $6 chinos and so forth. In the sixties.

The gals, photographed in my apartment.
From left: Louise Savitt, Topsy Taylor McFadden,
Chessy Rayner, Missy Bancroft. Front: Mica Ertegun.

FROM LEFT: *Barbara Walters, Casey Ribicoff, Mica Ertegun, Nina Griscom, Nan Kempner, Pat Buckley, Carolyne Roehm, Duane Hampton, and Marguerite Littman.*

Hearing of Stanley Marcus's death today [January 22, 2002], I am reminded that Slim won the Neiman Marcus Award, back in 1946. This might not be significant if Slim, then in her late twenties and living in California (and soon to marry Leland Hayward) weren't the first person outside the fashion industry to receive the award. It was Slim's original look—the informal men's wardrobe of plaid shirts and cowboy pants or a black sweater with the sleeves pushed up and her hair tied simply back—that Carmel Snow wanted when she had her photographed in *Harper's Bazaar* wearing her own clothes. It was a totally American kind of glamour. And you have to remember, at that point, everybody important was dressed by somebody. But Slim had no affiliations. She did it herself. Later on, when she was living in New York, in the fifties, Mainbocher made her some things. I imagine she came to him through her friend Babe, or Mary Martin, who was dressed by Mainbocher both on and off the stage, or Kitty Miller, one of his original shareholders. I first met Slim, briefly, at one of Kitty's cocktail parties.

By the sixties, as word got around, more women were coming in. Mica was coming in. Nan Kempner and Mrs. Buckley. Nancy Kissinger started coming in during the seventies. Nancy and Henry played a huge role in my social life in the eighties and nineties, inviting me to their parties in Washington and New York. It was really the Kissingers, I found out later, who were responsible for inviting me to my first state dinner at the White House, in 1976, during Queen Elizabeth's Bicentennial visit. That was the hottest ticket—and the hottest night—in Washington. Absolutely sweltering. I took Slim, who wore a strapless chiffon dress in shades of pink and peach that I had made for her, and we went with Jack and Dru Heinz. You couldn't take your eyes off the guests that night. It was the most incredible throng. Cary Grant was there. Alice Roosevelt Longworth. The heads of every big industry. But would you believe that not a single individual from the fashion world had been included on the original guest list? It was the Kissingers who saw the gaffe. And I must say I enjoyed the head-spinning symmetry of being introduced by President Ford to the Queen of England "as our king of fashion." Granted the title was by default and the euphoria would evaporate by Monday morning, but don't kid yourself: All designers love those rare occasions when they are the only one.

*Nancy Kissinger at
one of my shows.*

When Nancy was first married to Henry, she was photographed every single day. I guess there were days when the press photographers took her picture at lunch *and* dinner. So she needed a lot of clothes. Being tall and racehorse thin, and blessed with those aristocratic looks that photograph, to this day, like a million, Nancy could wear extreme clothes. Not flashy: gutsy. One thing I made for her was a gray cashmere jersey suit, to the floor, with lynx cuffs and an off-white satin blouse. It was a fabulous look on her for evening, and so different from the way everyone else was dressed.

Annette is true blue. Not changed a hair since we first met in the early sixties, when she was married to Sam Reed. Men adore Annette for the simple reason that she excites them—with her mind, her knowledge of books, her spitfire conversation. She became great friends with Tim Healy, and really stood up for him when liberals were saying he was going to destroy the Public Library because he was a Jesuit. She always looks her best in a Saint Laurent pantsuit with just a T-shirt and her hair pulled back; but, like Nancy, she loves any excuse to dress up at night—the bigger the skirt the better. One thing certainly about

*Annette de la Renta
getting a hug from Brutus.*

Annette is her capacity for friendship. She doesn't give friendship easily, but those who have it, from the time they were in school together, like Betsy Gotbaum, still have it today. And I think that's saying an awful lot in our society, when we tend to change friends several times in life.

ANNETTE DE LA RENTA: **Bill and I were talking yesterday [June 15, 2001] that Brooke is going to be one hundred next March. He had just had tea with her and I had picked her up from something at the Morgan Library. In the car she said, "He's agreed to do the most wonderful thing. He's going to design a dress for me and I want Oscar to make it." When I saw Oscar that night, I said, "Bill is going to send you a drawing and you're going to be making a dress for Brooke." And Oscar was laughing. He said, "I always wanted to do Bill's clothes."**

*At the Plaza,
late sixties. The
back belongs to
Nan Kempner.*

I just can't imagine a time when Nan wasn't around. Maybe that's because I've known her for so long. And I always preferred to be alone with her,
just the two of us for lunch, rather than with a group. She's good company, and
howlingly funny. Her great appeal to designers, of course, is her total involve-
ment in fashion. I've never forgotten how supportive she was of me when I first
started going out to San Francisco. Because, in San Francisco, Nan is something
of an object of reverence. They've never had anybody leave for the real world,
and really establish themselves, at least in fashion. I remember being at a dinner party in London with the Andrewses, who are also from San Francisco, and
one of the guests was speaking against Nan. "Ah, that dreadful woman." And,
boy, did Emma Andrews let her have it. She said, "You have no right to speak
about my friend that way. You obviously don't know that Nan is one of the kind-
est, most generous people. She's none of the things you're saying she is." The
other woman was so taken aback. And all those years when I was going out to

I am with Pat Buckley at a Literary Lions dinner at the New York Public Library.

San Francisco or Lake Tahoe for shows, Nan would always be there. That's not exactly like popping down to Washington. There have been times when her stock has not been very high. But that was just overexposure. One thing about Nan is she's not petty.

NAN KEMPNER: **You can put Saint Laurent and Bill on the same plane in a way—their clothes go forever. Bill's attitude, and the attitude of his clothes, was "knock it off." The clothes always had a really American cool look. Glamour he gave, but it was the easiest kind—a gray flannel coat lined in gray squirrel. Or a raincoat lined in the same tweed as the suit to go under it.**

Women like Nan and Pat Buckley tended to approach dressing as a business. Strip down to their bras and pantyhose and stand there smoking a cigarette.* Pat just loved being in her pantyhose and bra. One day in the middle of a fitting, Chip Rubinstein, who was Anne Klein's husband, came by and I stuck my head out to say, "Hi, Chip." Mrs. Buckley, naturally, wanted to know who Chip was, and I said, "You don't know him." And dressed like that, she went to the door and said, "Hi, Chip." A provocateur.

I remember once Mrs. Buckley and I were in Brussels with Carol Price, and Carol, whose husband was the ambassador to England, was on her way to meet him in Nassau. She had about seven steamer trunks of clothes in her room. Her room—forget it. Anyway, for some reason her secretary couldn't get through to Carol's room—she had been trying for hours—so I said I'd knock on her door, and I asked Pat to come with me. So Pat said, "I'll put my robe on." All of her robes are of the Victoria's Secret type. And since their average size is for someone four or five inches shorter than she is, that leaves a lot of Pat exposed.

We went and knocked on Carol's door: "Who is it, who is it?"

I said, "Carol, it's Bill. I have to talk to you."

We waited, and waited, and waited. I knew Carol wouldn't come to the door until she was completely dressed and had her hair in tip-top order. All that diplomatic training. I adore Carol. She is one of the most devoted friends. But by this point a group of Japanese tourists was passing through the hall—and there was Mrs. Buckley, with her long martini legs swirling out from that shorty robe, half naked.

I've never had as much fun with anyone in my life as I've had with Mrs. Buckley. In the first place, she makes fun of herself, which is the best kind of humor. But also, funny things happen to her that don't happen to other people. I was in a stretch limo with her once, and as I turned to help her out—we both had been drinking a bit, I may add—she came out on all fours. She said, "I can't stand up in here. So I have to come out this way." I took her to the first Reagan inaugural; Bill Buckley was there, too. We went to a party that Nancy Whitehead

---

*My first experience with this sort of casual intimacy was in the early sixties during a fitting with Marilyn Monroe. MM didn't bother with underwear at all. She and Arthur Miller lived in my building, at 444, and one day Norman Norell, who had recently made Monroe some clothes but was on his way to Europe, asked me if I would make her a last-minute skirt and blouse. The fitting took place in her apartment. Most women are more concerned about how they will look on top; Monroe is the only woman I ever met who gave all her attention to her derriere. She knew exactly what those seams should do. And she couldn't have been sweeter. But poor David Evins. The shoemaker used to get so flustered when he went for a fitting.

was giving, and as we stood in the coat line, I noticed that Pat had suddenly vanished. I got up to the hat check, and there she was. She had fallen and was behind the counter.

I said, "What in the world . . ."

"He pushed me!"

I turned around. It was Bill Simon, the secretary of defense.

PAT BUCKLEY: **Bill and I had a thing that we would do two or three times a year. It took the planning of D-Day. We'd see five movies in a day. We'd start out at nine o'clock in the morning to catch the ten o'clock show. Very often we'd catch lunch from an umbrella cart on the corner. Then we'd drag ourselves home around midnight. It was so much fun and we'd laugh ourselves sick.**

Someone else I used to take to the movies a lot was Vreeland. Diana adored going to the movies, and those were the evenings I loved most with her. Though I often went to her apartment for dinner, alone or with Mrs. Buckley, I rarely escorted Diana to dinners, because, as everyone knew, she was always late. Kitty Miller, who lived in the same building as Diana, had a rule about sitting down at 8:45. And if Vreeland wasn't there, we sat down without her. She never had a sense of time, and I don't think it was that ploy of being important when she arrived. Time, like age, simply meant nothing to her.

Her apartment was really minuscule. It had a drawing room, done in red, clutter everywhere; and at the end of the room was a small sitting room, with bookcases and a banquette, where dinner would be served. Reed planned all the menus, and the food was always simple but delicious. When I first met the Vreelands, in the fifties, it was actually Reed who was friendlier. Astonishingly friendly when you consider that the stigma of being a designer was enough to make you feel like an outcast. And then there were the more conventional social hurdles, such as where one had gone to school. I remember Tommy Bancroft telling me, in this same period, that he didn't make a single friend after he had left prep school. We got on terrifically. He had never met anybody like me, and I had never met anybody like him. But the two men who showed me exceptional kindness, in terms of letting me in, were Reed and Serge Obolensky. Dashingly handsome, with a thin mustache, Serge was the first or second of Alice Astor's four husbands—Alice Bouverie, in the end.

I saw more of Diana after Reed's death. What did we talk about? What we are talking about now: people. People are generally more interesting than the clothes they make.

Diana herself was not of a piece, however. She was an amalgam of stories and half-truths and outright lies that served her ideal, and which sometimes seemed a charade, but in New York, amid kindred souls, was utterly comprehended. And for that reason, despite her Paris birth, her love of French clothes, her polished soles, her frequent evocations of Chanel, Bébé Bérard, and Queen Mary—all those things we have come to associate with this vague antique world of Vreelandia—I think Diana was deeply American. She combined Twain's reverence for the reinvented self with Barnum's love of showmanship, and she spent her life perfecting this blend. The cranelike walk, the kabuki makeup, the exaggerated gestures—how else could a chic woman without beauty have stood out in fashionable New York? And not only that, be the leading fashion arbiter of her time? It must have saved her from disappointment many times, this surrealist conception of herself. For I don't think Diana's great skills as an editor had anything to do with her understanding of culture or her talent for succinctly expressing its mood with terms like "youthquake" or "the beautiful people." Rather, it had to do with something more powerful, more innate, a belief held in common with others who had been born outside New York and which had saved them, too, on many occasions—and that was her perception of herself. Diana saw the world through her own eyes, and that was truth enough for her.

Another who grandly dispensed with conventional truth was the designer Valentina. I used to love talking to her. She had led such a fascinating life with her husband, George Schlee, in Russia and Paris, right after the First War; and then Garbo entered their lives, as George's friend. You'd see her at their cocktail parties. Valentina was the model for everything she designed—in every sense. The fact that Katharine Hepburn wore her clothes in the stage version of *The Philadelphia Story* and set off a wave of demand that kept the Schlees in hay for years—fine. But Valentina really made clothes to suit herself. She once came out

Casey and Abe Ribicoff.

with a perfume called My Own, which tells you everything. I don't remember how My Own smelled, but I'm sure it didn't smell like anyone else's perfume. I think a woman should have an identifiable scent, and it should precede her into a room. That way, when she gets off the lift, people will say, "Here comes Emily." I think that's all right.

But do you know what I remember most about Valentina? The way she took care of herself—her hands, her hair, her makeup. Everything immaculate. She treated herself as if she was the most special piece of porcelain. And it wasn't a matter of being narcissistic.

It's funny how certain words go in and out of vogue. In the sixties, the dirtiest word in fashion was "wearable." Nobody wanted to be known for wearable clothes, although I was. Now the whole thing has reversed, and it's "chic" and "elegant," which are passé. This is understandable. Because although there are many well-turned-out women today—Blaine Trump, Anna Wintour, Brooke de O'Campo, Reinaldo and Carolina Herrera's* daughters, Patricia and Carolina, come to mind—there is very little consistency. And the chic of a Babe Paley was based totally on consistency of line. It demanded incredible dedica-

---

*Clearly, in the case of the Herreras, style is hereditary. Before Carolina went into business, I made clothes for her and her mother-in-law, Mimi. Mimi was an extraordinary beauty: white skin, black hair, often dressed by Balenciaga. I still recall arriving at the airport for another road show and seeing what looked like a beaming light of a miracle amid that jet-lagged humanity. That's the effect of Carolina's glamour. Her humor, on the other hand, is of the earth: low and delicious.

At darts wih the designer Gus Tassell and others.

tion, and years of standing in fitting rooms. "Make the sleeve a quarter inch shorter . . ." And that's not important anymore. It's not important to be chic.

Until I began this book, I had forgotten how many of my friends, especially in the fifties and sixties, were European. Serge, Valentina, Tiff, Niki, of course. Obviously, running through us, fueled by wit and laughter, was the common denominator of style—nevertheless, I was an American designer, all my inclinations and experiences were American, and though this occasionally put me on the outs with editors, all my success came from looking through this one window.

But, as I say, it's a big country out there, and you never know who you are going to meet . . .

NAN KEMPNER: **When Bill showed up in another town, it was like the second coming of Christ. No matter where he went, he had friends and he made more with each trip. He was fun and interested, and interesting. Some of his comments about those trips were pretty interesting, too, and if the ladies knew what he said, they slit his throat. But that's our Bill.**

7

When Everything Was Personal

The summer I left home for New York I said good-bye to Jockey, my black-and-tan terrier mix, not knowing how many years lay ahead of me before I would again have the moral support of a dog and his drool on my pillow. A dog is good company, sometimes the best company, but it wasn't until I bought my house in Connecticut, in 1976, that I had enough space and trees for a dog. The first to arrive was a pair of golden retriever litter mates I named Brutus and Kate. I really loved Kate. She was affectionate and loyal to her dying day; yet she never hovered with fake solicitude. She pursued her own line of superior interests, be it a rotten apple or a frog disgorged from a storm drain. Shelby was the next golden retriever, and she had Kate's same qualities except in reverse proportion. She was a sufferer, the classic middle child. Our trouble was she arrived while the other pups still crowded my loyalties, so we never had a proper bonding period.

Nowadays my affections, and most of my bed, are taken up by a blond and boxy Labrador named Barnaby, whose thick, many creased neck you want to roughly cuddle. Barnaby's idea of activity is to go and stand sentry for a half hour by the front gate, and once he is satisfied the perimeter is secure, go for a dip in the pool. Cocking his head slightly to the right, he pretends to give a sympathetic hearing to everything I have to say, and only once has he let me down—

and then under circumstances that would have desperately tested any dog. Barnaby and I had been invited to have Christmas Eve dinner with Annette and Oscar de la Renta at their home in Kent, where they had just added a new wing for their bed-sitting room. Brooke Astor was there with her little dachshund and schnauzer. Carolyne Roehm had her four dogs. The Kissingers were there with their Lab. And, of course, Annette had her terriers. Don't ask me how many dogs that was. It was cozy. Annette had set up the tree at the end of the room, with a nativity scene under it. There were carols and fun presents for everyone. And then, in the middle of all this, Barnaby went over to the tree and lifted his leg. Bang! There went two of the three wise men.

When Annette and I got done howling—and one thing about Annette is she has a great sense of the ridiculous—I said, "But Barnaby never does that." Well, she thought it was hilarious. I mean, whoever thought of putting a crèche under a Christmas tree . . .

I have known Oscar, as I say, since the first month he arrived in New York, in 1962, from Paris, where he had been Castillo's assistant at Lanvin. Oscar was a bit shy, but immensely good-looking, suntanned, with a lot more hair on his head than he has now, and a slight stutter—though, I think, even this women find appealing in a man. And women were enticed by Oscar. But he didn't know many people when he came here, to work for Elizabeth Arden, though he soon met C.Z. and Winston Guest. One day she invited Oscar for lunch, then she asked him for a weekend; pretty soon he had his own room at Templeton and was going every weekend. It was through C.Z. that Oscar met Bill and Babe Paley. Later, a group of us—Mica and Ahmet Ertegun, Chessy and Bill Rayner, Marella Agnelli, Jerry Robbins, Slim, and myself—would go down to Oscar's place in Santo Domingo, when the country was still as primitive as you can imagine. By then, he had married his first wife, Françoise de Langlade, a former editor of French *Vogue*.

The sixties in fashion wouldn't have worked out the way it did—or become the great American decade—without three people coming to power almost at the same time: John Fairchild, who returned to New York in 1960 to run his family's trade paper; Diana Vreeland, who took over *Vogue* in 1962; and Eugenia Sheppard, who started her "Inside Fashion" column in the *Herald Tribune* almost as a wastebin to catch the stuff that other reporters were ignoring at the 1956 wedding

of Prince Rainier and Grace Kelly. By 1962, Eugenia was so good at this kind of reporting, which involved nothing more than gathering great details and telling them with a point of view, that *Newsweek* wrote a column about *her*.

And another thing: None of these journalists was exactly proletariat in opinion or background. This was important. Despite the insistence on youth in fashion, and the invasion of British working-class models and photographers, like Twiggy and David Bailey, New York society was still dominated by various elitist institutions—Wall Street, primarily, but also the museum boards, the April in Paris ball, and Elsie Woodward's drawing room. John had gone to Princeton. Diana had been brought up eccentrically in Europe before her marriage to Reed, a banker. Eugenia, who came from Columbus, Ohio, had gone to Bryn Mawr and was married to Walter Millis, a newspaperman and military historian. They lived at the Dakota, where Jean vanden Heuvel, her sister Susan Stein, the Carter Burdens, Jason Robards and Lauren Bacall also had apartments, and where, of course, the term "radical chic" came into vogue one night in January 1970, when the Bernsteins gave their party for the Black Panthers.

Eugenia knew all these people. Walter had no interest in society, so she left him at home, night after night. And after Walter died, she took up with Earl Blackwell, the founder of Celebrity Register. What she loved beyond anything else in the world was to dance, and would dance all night if somebody asked her. And then she'd write about who she saw out that night. I made clothes for her sometimes and she didn't want anything conservative. She wanted feathers. And you've got to picture her—this tiny thing, not much more than five feet, if that. When she got into her station wagon to drive—and she was in her eighties then—it looked like a car coming down the road with nobody in it. And then you'd see these little blond curls just above the steering wheel.

Dancing with Eugenia.

With Gloria Vanderbilt and Claudette Colbert.

As soon as John arrived back in New York, he and I started meeting for lunch once a week, usually at the St. Regis, a custom we continued, except for one or two brief cooling-off periods, for more than thirty years, until he retired. I've kept all my date books, going back to 1970, so I know where I was every weekday at one o'clock, and with whom. I don't mention this to brag—it seems scarcely worth bragging about—but merely to emphasize how important the restaurant lunch became in the sixties. People started going two and three times a week to La Caravelle or La Grenouille, and later the Four Seasons, not only because the food was so delicious, but also to check out who was there and what they were wearing. That had been the point of El Morocco, too, but suddenly it was the unexpected intimacy of seeing Jackie Kennedy at lunch with her sister, or Gloria Vanderbilt Cooper and Babe Paley with their friends, that John picked up on when he started referring to them just as Jackie, Gloria, and Babe. And don't forget the country was just coming out of the deep snore of Eisenhowerism, when prosperity, combined with mass-produced fulfillment—television, Levittown, the blossoming of the golden arches—led to the biggest consumer spending spree in history. But it was taste based on conformity and economic

With Chessy Rayner and Mica Ertegun, the founders of MAC II.

contentment, not individuality. And after 1960, everything would become personal. And frenetic.

One day in the early sixties, John and I were having lunch at La Caravelle with Luis Estevez, a designer of that era, when John said something to the effect: Why not get designers to talk frankly about fashion and each other? John later said I choked on my artichoke leaf, but I think I was just distracted by Charlotte Ford walking past, with the ex-Mrs. Henry Ford II in a fitted black Givenchy suit. Well, Luis, who was Cuban and a sexy individual, was all for it. The following Monday morning he gave an interview from his bed. He spared nothing, beginning with the first line: "The fashion world is phony." After that, John just kept raising the bar, and everybody scrambled under it. Though for some people, especially eager socialites, the process was more like going through

VOGUE

NOV
$3.00

**Brilliant
New
Ways**
to Look
at Night

The Body Is Back
*How Do You
Measure Up?*

Talk Dirty to Me:
Sallie Tisdale's Day
in a Sex Shop

**Four-Star
Turkey**
By Jeffrey Steingarten

**Whom Do
Women
Really
Dress For?**

PLUS
Glenn Close

Soft wear:
coats
warm up

Hardware:
accessories
strike gold

a car wash in reverse: They didn't come out clean.* But John, with childlike simplicity—and the experience of covering big cats like Chanel—recognized that there was no fantasy quotient to be found in the lives of manufacturers. So he focused on the designers, finding out about them personally, and empathetically removing the grubby backroom taint of Seventh Avenue by treating us, frankly, as stars.

Of course, it helped that one had something amusing to offer John, because he was really like a voyeur at those lunches. He was like a little boy: *Tell me more* . . . Someone who was formidable at telling everything was Jacques Tiffeau. His information was truly keyhole quality, attended with the zest of Julia Child spooning out a pot au feu. Hardly anyone remembers the name Tiffeau today, nor does it appear much in fashion books, even in biographies of Dior, though it was Jacques, along with Madame Raymond, Dior's legendary *directrice*, who inherited much of his personal fortune. But Tiff was among a handful of European and Latin American designers who arrived in New York at the end of the fifties, and had a great deal to do, I think, with making American fashion exciting in the era of the so-called Beautiful People. Another was Ferdinando Sarmi, a Roman count who had a flair for evening clothes. How did Sarmi end up in New York? Money. There was no one in Paris in the early sixties to match the chic vitality, and spending power, of Jackie,† Gloria, and Babe—or Jane Holzer, Isabel Eberstadt, and Susan Stein, who was the daughter of Jules Stein. Paris was old bags. So Tiff, who possessed talent (he made all his first samples himself) as well as sexual bravura, moved here, and soon he became one of John's regular noontime confidants. I think Tiff made up half the stuff he told John, just to titillate him. But John admired Tiffeau's spunk, and I think you can understand how John lost interest in Norell after initially building him up. Norell may have been God's left hand in terms of talent, but once John discovered there was no *life* there—only the excitement around the table at Schrafft's—he stopped

---

*Though she belongs to the eighties, Susan Gutfreund is the obvious example. After I described one of her lavish parties to John ("Every chair twined in roses. Beautiful, even though the thorns sometimes stuck in your back or caught the ladies' hair . . ."), he started writing about Susan, dubbing her the Mother of Nouvelle Society, even calling her silly. In spite of this, they are friends today.

† As reported by Marylin Bender, the expert sleuth Charlotte Curtis of the *New York Times* painstakingly calculated that Mrs. Kennedy spent $50,000 on her clothes in the first sixteen months after the election.

WHEN EVERYTHING WAS PERSONAL

John Fairchild.

writing about Norell. Norman got as mad as hell about that, but there was nothing he could do. He was out.

Over the years friends have remarked that they thought John deliberately played Oscar off me, and vice versa, in an attempt to keep both of us off balance, especially in the eighties, when Wall Street money kept everybody a little unsteady with wonder and nausea. There might be some truth to the complaint. Certainly Oscar and I held a similar promontory view of things, and the fact that we knew the same people, went to the same parties, and were—are—friends without being serious rivals would have uniquely exposed one or both of us to John's deflationary zeal. *Tell me more* . . . zap! And it did happen from time to time. But not for reasons, I knew, that were personal.

JOHN FAIRCHILD: **It was very simple. You favored them the way the clothes were made. I think Bill is a much more authentic designer than Oscar, and that's what we based our judgment on. Bill is an American designer. He was much more attuned to American life than Norell or Galanos. I used to tell him all the time: "Stick to your great American look." He was better at it than anyone else.**

I didn't get to know Oscar well until after he and Françoise were married, in 1967. They bought their place up in Kent, because of Alex and Tatiana Liberman, who had a house nearby, and I often stayed with them. The marriage was made in heaven. They had the same goals, and she worked twenty-four hours a day, every day, helping Oscar with his career. She had known everyone in Paris, and in a very short time, she got to know everybody in New York. She made no bones about the fact that she wanted famous names at her dinner parties. She wanted the Windsors, she wanted Irene Selznick, she wanted Baryshnikov and Nureyev. And in a way she was correct. People were never bored at her house. She had good food and she entertained beautifully, even though they didn't have a nickel in those days.

Perhaps the most striking fact of the sixties was just how little money any of us had. When I began this book, I expected to offer some pleading explanation of why I felt so out of it in the sixties, mostly having to do with youth being a new class (to quote Roger Vadim) and how, at forty-three (my age in 1965), I felt too old to seriously picture myself twisting the night away at the Peppermint Lounge in a tiger-print shirt. And never mind that my friendships were neatly parted between those who were twenty years younger than I (Louise and Missy), and those who had really crossed over (Niki and Kitty). The sixties was cruelly demographic. Yet in going through my archives, as well as those of Condé Nast and Hearst, I see that I was much looser than I had remembered. My hand has always begun to sketch the moment it hits the page—and you see this. You see it in the ecstatic lace daisies of a white baby-doll dress, circa 1968.

No, for me, the clarifying detail of the sixties was my salary: $1,000 per week. And that was at the *end* of the sixties. Clearly, with a valet in my employ and a closet full of bespoke suits, I managed—and I was single, and there were the odd perks* of increasing visibility. But it points up something you commonly don't catch in the hyperventilating about youth in the sixties—and that is, how modest

*The oddest of these now comes in the form of a small but gratifying monthly pension from the Screen Actors Guild. Advertisers in the sixties discovered the snob appeal of having a designer appear in television commercials for products other than clothes, and often without identifying him. The implication was: If you don't know him, you don't get it. I was the first designer to do such commercials. Hence, my SAG pension. Once, in the fifties, I was offered a screen test. This was the heyday of actors like Van Johnson—guys who were not necessarily talented but had screen appeal. Well, I couldn't see how that would enhance my career, and I declined.

life was, too. People would have wonderful cocktail parties, like Josh and Nedda Logan, who lived around the corner from me, at 435 East 52nd Street, in a big apartment overlooking the East River, all bright lights in and out; yet you didn't go there to ogle the stars, and certainly nobody went with a thought of networking, the way people do now. You went to have fun. I used to have small dinners at my place: six or seven people, drinks on the terrace, maybe lamb chops. I was in the middle of cooking one such dinner the night of the first blackout. Or, Kitty would phone and say, "You know, I never get steak tartare in New York," and the following Thursday night, she'd come over and I'd fix her steak tartare with the raw egg and everything, capers on the side. Someone else I saw a lot of in those days was Kit Gill, a lanky blond model who personified the sporty, I-don't-give-a-damn style I liked—all clean hair and a touch of charm-school insolence. One day she presented herself to me in my office and said, "I'm Katherine Gill." I said, "No, you're not. You're Kit." Well, she looked like a Kit. Later she married Louise's brother, Bobby Liberman, whose mother was Ruth Tankoos. I know everyone says this sort of thing, but it *was* a small world.

Oscar and Françoise had their place in Santo Domingo—this must have been in the early seventies—and a group of us would go down over Christmas. Though small, their place was luxurious compared to the rest of the country, and one sensed the political troubles. It's the only time I've been to a nightclub, where, in addition to the hatcheck girl, you had to have someone to stow the machine guns. So many of the guests had guns with them. Since Oscar and Françoise had only a couple of bedrooms in those days, the rest of us bunked at a local motel. We used to sit in the parking lot, waiting for our rides, and I remember sitting out there one morning, like this, getting the sun, and saying, "If anyone would ever tell me I'd come all this distance to get the sun in a fucking parking lot, I'd say you were crazy." But everyone loved those trips, and Françoise's food was always so good. The girls—Slim, Mica, Chessy—would lie around in their caftans, wearing the turbans that Madame Grès had shown them how to tie. One night in Santo Domingo, at one of those clubs where there was a man to receive your gun, the Erteguns and I gave a dinner, using the motel bedspreads as tablecloths.

In Santo Domingo with Slim, Zip, the Rayners, and the Erteguns.

OSCAR DE LA RENTA: **Slim told me this story. She and Bill were
dancing, and she was sort of putting her hands around him.
It was a beautiful night, with the moon, and she said to him,
"This is a perfect night to fall in love." And he said, "Well, this
is the most perfect night, the most beautiful moon and music.
But the wrong guy to fall in love with."**

I got to know the Logans when Nedda started coming up to buy clothes
from me, and then Josh and I became friends. I used to go out to the Golden Door,
for the men-only weeks, in the seventies and eighties, joined by the same group of
guys from around the country, and Josh came with me once or twice. I remember
we mapped out an entire story involving ways to murder people at a spa—"Death
at the Golden Door." Not exactly *Mister Roberts*, but we laughed like hell. Josh was
a good old boy, a great slob. He was a manic-depressive, of course—miserably unhappy, though Nedda was the ideal woman to have as his partner. They gave great
parties. Everybody came, from Mrs. Woodward to Betty Comden and Adoph

Green. Jule Styne was there. Fifty people would come through, and they were from all facets of society; certainly anyone who was in town from Hollywood. You'd see Truman Capote,* a senator from Washington, Jimmy Stewart. People you wouldn't see at ordinary cocktail parties. Their parties were simply a remarkable occasion to bring people together and have a good time.

The actress Louise Allbritton was another who really made that era fun. She was married to Charles Collingwood, the ace CBS broadcaster. He was a handsome man and she was beautiful and often drunk. We became great pals. They were living in London, on Eaton Square, when I first knew them; later they lived on East 57th Street, across from me. I remember taking Ruth Tankoos to dinner at their home in London, and just like that, I saw a spark happen between Charles and Ruth. I don't know if Louise noticed it or not. But the room went absolutely—well, it was a spark. I saw a lot of Louise after they moved to New York. One night I had her over to dinner with Tiffeau. She had on a blouse, and Tiffeau said, "I hate that." With that, he grabbed it and tore it off her. And Louise didn't have a bra on. She just sort of shimmied out of the remains of the blouse and sat there through the rest of the dinner, naked from the waist up. Wouldn't even acknowledge that Tiffeau had done it. He did a similar thing at another dinner of mine, with Ruth and a whole group of people present. He took off his clothes. He did have a good body. But I just loved that Ruth pretended he was as dressed as anybody. She was actually crazy about Jacques.

Anyway, the next day Louise and I were on the phone. She said, "Wouldn't you think he'd have the decency to send me a blouse?" Knowing Jacques, who probably had the first dollar he'd ever earned, I said, "Don't expect it." Cheap. *Mmm.*

I've been trying to figure out what to say about Tiff. All of us who knew him loved him. We loved the richness and daring-do of his personality in an era when personality—not youth, not money, but *personality*—ventilated fashion. Of course, he lived on the edge, way out on the edge for most of us, but that, too, was part of the fascination. He arrived in this country from the Loire Valley in France, literally off the farm—no money, no connections—and made it. He was

*Mention of Truman brings to mind the late and hilarious Patrick O'Higgins, a half-French, half-Irish journalist who was secretary to Helena Rubinstein. He was working on a book about her life when Truman came out with *In Cold Blood*. Patrick wanted to call her book *In Cold Cream*. Miss Rubinstein was not amused. But I'd hate for it to get away.

sitting at a tailor's bench, in New York, at the coat-and-suit firm of Monte-Sano & Pruzan, when Sophie Gimbel brought in Christian Dior one day. And I guess the old boy went gaga when he saw this proud, robust-looking guy sitting astride that bench. But Tiff would have made it on his own, and did, with a successful label called Tiffeau & Busch. I imagine what fated us to be friends was that neither one of us had, by choice, many designers as close friends. And there was the treacherous but irresistible pitch of his humor, so bawdily like an American's, and so brazenly dispensed.

One night I took him to see *Oh, Calcutta!* soon after it had opened. We had very good seats, in the front row, and as we craned our necks upward, he said, "Gee, Bilbo, we may not be able to see everything, but we sure can smell everything." He said it in a loud voice, too.

But Tiffeau would also point up the vulnerability of friendship. Whatever I can, and will, say about this boundless, irreverent figure must be tempered by the fact that he is the only friend who ever betrayed me. Sometime in the mid-seventies, when Tiff was again living in Paris and had more or less burned the last of his bridges—he had worked for Saint Laurent, Balmain, even Guy Laroche and been fired from all for one excess or another—he phoned me up and asked if he could return to New York to design my Blassport collections. Blassport was being manufactured by a licensee with whom I warily but successfully did business. Given the unscrupulousness of Seventh Avenue, and Tiff's humor and evergreen talent, I thought it would be a good idea to have him on my side, so I told him: "Yes. Come back to New York."

The first couple of collections were fine. Then one day in the middle of the third, he called and asked if we could meet that afternoon at my apartment. That should have been the tip-off—choosing a place where nobody else would be around—but I don't remember thinking anything of it. As soon as he walked into the apartment, however, he burst into what seemed to be premeditated tears. Then it came out: He and the manufacturer were going to take over Blassport. They were taking it away from me.

Tearfully, he said, "I hate to do it, Bilbo, but it's my chance."

Though I am not sentimental, I would have preferred it to have gone the other way. I would have preferred our friendship to go on forever. But that's not how it worked out. I said, "I think you'd better go." Blassport remained with me for at least another decade, until it went out of existence. Jacques returned to Paris, where he died ten years later. Lung cancer—he was a four-pack-a-day man.

Why did he do it? Not for money. Do you know that every year on his birthday Madame Raymond gave him a gold brick? I think there was just a strain in that big wicked personality of his that made him want to destroy things, including himself.

But I must admit that his plan to take over Blassport showed characteristic spunk. He and the manufacturer already had stationery printed with the new name. It was to be called "SporTiff."

8

On the Road

It was the late summer of 1974 and I had just come from giving a fashion show in the art center in Little Rock, a city that now resonates as the locus of much prepresidential Clinton sexual scandal. Or "bimbo eruptions," as I believe his handlers called it later. Chiefly out of partisan curiosity—I am a Republican except on the few occasions when I've thought it sounder to vote democrat (FDR, JFK)—I went back to one of his biographies (Maraniss: *First in His Class*), and I see that Clinton was in Little Rock at the time of my visit, although nowhere near the governor's mansion; he was running for a congressional seat. I was then doing some aggressive stumping of my own on the fashion and trunk show circuit. Fashion shows have been around, in one form or another, in this country since 1914, when Edna Woolman Chase, the editor of *Vogue*, delicately browbeat Mrs. Vincent Astor, Mrs. Stuyvesant Fish, and Mrs. William K. Vanderbilt, among other best-dressed society ladies, into serving as patronesses of her first Fashion Fete, where a handful of *Vogue* secretaries went through the motions of French mannequins. Now, of course, fashion shows go on for *weeks*, on practically every continent, and everybody imitates each other.

But apart from the gold-chair salon showings that designers gave for their private clients and the press, it was still a novelty in the late fifties, when I started going on the road, for a designer to travel with his collection to another

On the road.

city. It was Lynn Manulis and her mother, Martha, who had the idea that I come meet their clients personally at their store in Palm Beach. They simply saw that having a designer around increased the traffic. And I liked getting out of New York. I'd go down for a couple of weeks a year and stay at the Colony Hotel, which was owned by Ruth Tankoos and her husband, Joe. Ruth was an amazing woman. Full of spunk and fun. She also owned 530 and 550 Seventh Avenue, where most of the better designers were quartered. I remember one day we were meeting for lunch at La Grenouille and the snowstorm of the century blew up. I phoned her and said, "You're not going out today for God's sake." She said, "Of course I am." She arrived at Grenouille wearing a pair of sling-back Chanel shoes and a white Chanel suit with a sable coat over her shoulders. The chauffeur practically carried her to the door. As she dropped onto the plush banquette, I said, "Honey, the rich really are different." I like somebody who isn't worried about the elements.

The grandes dames of Hobe Sound and Palm Beach, such as Madame Jacques Balsan, the former Consuelo Vanderbilt, couldn't have cared less about

WWD photo by LOUISE J. ESTERHAZY

AUTO-EROTICISM: **Bill Blass**, the designer, as he appeared in a Palm Beach parking lot one recent afternoon.

meeting a backroom designer from New York; in fact, Martha would open her shop early for Madame Balsan so she could get what she needed and leave. But the younger women were intrigued, if not already changing the style of Palm Beach. And they were always looking for the extra man, etc. I became good friends with two of the friendliest of the bunch: Flo Pritchard, who had a local society column and was married to Earl E. T. Smith, and Alice Topping. Slim Aarons did a famous portrait of Alice lying by a pool in Palm Beach wearing a white cotton bathing suit and a gray T-shirt. It's in his book *A Wonderful Time*.

By the mid-seventies, after a martini here and there, I was traveling thirty thousand miles a year. There was hardly an American city, or a group of gals, I didn't know. Washington, Nashville, Detroit, Chicago, Seattle, San Francisco, Los Angeles, Phoenix, Dallas, Houston. I was in Midland, Texas, for a trunk show when a woman was trying on some clothes and a cow stuck its head—*her* head—through the dressing-room window. Another time, in El Paso, the manager of the Saks store asked me if I'd like to have dinner that evening across the border in Nogales at the home of a client.

With Helen O'Hagan, my frequent consort on the road.

"I want you to see the house," the manager said, "because he's the biggest tomato grower in the world, and he has a beautiful place."

I'll never forget it. To get to the house, you went down this alley with chickens running around. Absolutely filthy. You stopped at a gate and you went through more gates, another courtyard, more incredible filth, and finally into one of the most beautiful homes I've ever seen. The man's mother, who didn't speak a word of English, was in Valentino, with a handbag over her arm. And the man himself was very personable, though he must have been doing more than grow tomatoes, because we found out a few weeks later that he had been murdered by his lover in Beverly Hills.

Usually on such trips I'd take Tom Fallon, and sometimes Gail Levenstein, from the office, or if it was for Saks, then Helen O'Hagan from their publicity department. These trips were not always as professional as they seem. Inevitably, there was the search for the food remembered from the last visit. The chicken hash in Boston. The white peaches in Tahoe, where for many summers

I did a show by the lake.* In Kansas City, it was a wonderful hamburger stand. Just as inevitably, though without the thrilling rush to my metabolism, was the media blitz. I'm not sure I can give anyone the vaguest idea of what it's like to encounter, in one day, thirty Japanese journalists filing separately into my room at the Okura in Tokyo. Normally with members of the press I give a kind of expert pantomime of myself—the tie askew, the cigarette going, some light verbal roughhousing. But that day I couldn't make a single stone skip. It's times like this when you realize how utterly incomprehensible American fashion can be to a foreign audience. Someone would ask me, "What is the inspiration for your collection?" I'd say, "Amish quilts," and the answer would come back, "Amish kilts." All day long it went on like this. And never mind trying to explain the difference. I just had to sit there and keep gassing away, while Gail, who was with me on that trip, went into the next room and quietly stuffed her face into the carpet to stop crying, from laughter.

So it is now the fall of 1974 and I am leaving the art center in Little Rock, where I've just given a show for Mrs. Winthrop Rockefeller's charity. Fallon is a few feet behind me, with the saleslady from our office, when out of the crowd steps a girl with long hair and wearing a white rayon blouse and a long black skirt. She looks like a cellist.

"Mr. Blass?"

I say, "Yes," smiling.

"I'd like to suck your cock," she says.

"Thank you very much, I'm so"—the words are already out of my mouth and now my arms are starting to flail around like a drowning man's— "uh . . . *FALLLONNN!*"

Fallon, who was watching this whole scene with mild curiosity, now says that my head jerked back so violently that his first thought was he couldn't imagine what I had said to this poor girl in her modest cello-playing outfit. What I had said? I was going to say "I'm so glad you liked the clothes," and rush on.

---

*Of all the road shows, this was my favorite. Everybody from San Francisco came: Charlotte Schultz, Dolph and Emma Andrews, Diana and Gorham Knowles, Sally and Warren Debenham, the columnist Herb Caen. We'd have box lunches at picnic tables; the runway would be along the shore. People with homes in Tahoe would arrive by boat. It had such a feeling of spontaneity, as if someone had said, "Hey, let's put on a fashion show." And the men got such a kick out of it. When there are husbands in the audience, the women get away with more—buying, that is.

Well, we do rush on. We go for ribs. Ribs are such a good thing to have before you go to bed. Thus loaded up, we return to our hotel, which is called the Camelot and features, among other amenities—super-sized guest suites—a direct view of the city jail. I get up to my room, open the door, and there she is.

"Oh, my God, what are you doing here?" I start to back out.

She makes a grab for my crotch. She's holding on as I'm backing out the door . . .

"This won't do . . . I'm calling security!"

She runs away as I get security on the phone. Well, they couldn't be more blasé about the situation. They say, "What can we do? She's got a key to every suite in the hotel." Apparently, she does this with all the famous guests. The odds are in her favor. There was a rock band staying at the hotel the week before.

By now, I'm out in the hall. It's after midnight and in the next room, a repairman is fixing a television set. You can see the lights blazing from the city jail.

I wait in Fallon's room for what seems an eternity and then go back to mine. It's a duplex, with the bedroom upstairs. So I go up—and, by God, she's up there. I run back down the stairs, out in the hall again—they're still working on the TV—and into Fallon's room. By now, we've got the saleslady up, too. The two of them come over to my room, check it out, wait another hour, and leave. The room is now double locked. I'm about to go to sleep when I hear a letter being slipped under the door. It is the filthiest letter. Telling me everything in pornographic detail that she would have done to me and what I had missed and so forth. The lewdest things you can imagine. Then she wrote: "P.S. I hated your daytime clothes."

The next morning, we're having breakfast in the coffee shop with a couple of the society ladies who are taking us to the airport, and I say, "Listen, that was some night I had." I give them the whole story.

Well, you'd think I was describing a trip to the supermarket. They couldn't be more blasé. "Oh, yeah," they say, "that's Connie—Little Rock Connie. She does this all the time, particularly with rock groups. There's an article about her in the latest *Cosmo*." One of them even runs over to the drugstore to get me a copy.

The advantages of having Fallon ride shotgun with me were evident not just in Little Rock or Nogales. In fact, when I first met him, in Paris, in 1967 at a party that Ruth Dubonnet was giving for the Duchess of Windsor, Fallon was doing his best to evade the amorous attentions of a French count. He was hiding in a corner. I was there that night with Zipkin and Stevie, it was around the time of the collections, and Zipkin, in that voice of his, had just finished saying, "Ruthie, who are all these terrible tradespeople you have in your home tonight?" when he saw Fallon and almost in the same breath said, "Who are you? You're adorable." Tom just has this easy ability to adapt to any situation, without hysteria or loss of ego. One night, years later—the seventies? the eighties?—he was taken to the opera and dinner by Sybil Harrington. Sybil was a great dame. Very crisp and petite and full of fun. Her late husband, Donald, had made a fortune in natural gas around Amarillo, Texas, and they had an apartment in the Sherry Netherland as well as a beautiful house in the Biltmore Estates in Phoenix, where I occasionally stayed on road trips. But Sybil had expectations toward me that, at least on my end, were never going to be met.

So Fallon took her out. And the first thing Sybil did when she got into the car was slip a bag of diamonds—bracelets, etc.—into his coat pocket, saying, "Darling, I didn't get to the safe. Keep these for me."

> TOM FALLON: **We go to dinner. Sybil has a couple of drinks and she says, "I just love Bill. That damn Lady Keith . . ." And so on. At one point she says, "I just want to throw my legs around him." Then she leans into me and says, "Of course, we all know you're the boyfriend." I set her straight about that, and she says, "Oh, thank God, *you're* not that way."**

I did shows outside the States, too—Brazil, Mexico, Japan, France, where we did a big presentation at the American embassy and, of course, the legendary group affair at Versailles, which was so horrible and monumental that almost nobody involved wanted to talk about it for years afterward. In 1975, I went to China at the invitation of the Chinese government. Halston had been their first choice. But when the Chinese emissaries came to see him in New York, he kept his dark glasses on. I guess that was considered very bad manners, and a very bad omen. They thought Halston was the devil. So they said, "He won't do." I was next on the list.

That was the first time I traveled, at least for business, with Jill and John Fairchild, whom I met in the early sixties when he was Paris bureau chief of *Women's Wear Daily*. Despite his complete seriousness about journalism, and his love of tomahawking vulnerable socialites, John is someone who just cannot resist a practical joke. One night in Tokyo, on another trip, he convinced Fallon and Emanuel Ungaro—not that it took much convincing—to climb out onto the roof of the Okura and try to scare me by tiptoeing up to my window. Except that I was waiting for them. Well, they made such a racket. And not only that, I was waiting for them in the nude. So they got an extra jolt when I whipped back the curtains.

But China . . . never have I loathed a place more than the land of a billion people. I thought I would never get out. Of course, this was right after Nixon

CLOCKWISE FROM TOP LEFT:
Brooke Astor; Nancy Reagan;
Nancy Kissinger; Lynn Wyatt;
after a show.

and Kissinger had opened the way to China. So the Chinese weren't used to seeing many foreign visitors, and the accommodations were still somewhat frugal. My main problem was I couldn't get enough to eat. The food was just . . . indescribable. Monkey brains and so forth. Jill and I got in the habit of meeting before dinner to have a whiskey and eat peanut butter and crackers—almost to the point, I think, where John felt excluded. That's another thing about John: Although he doesn't care much for society himself, he has to know everything that's going on.

JOHN FAIRCHILD: **One night in Canton, this very important Chinese lady, in charge of textiles or something, invites us to a banquet. We went with three of her men. Well, Bill got absolutely bombed on mai tais. I got the hiccups. And Bill keeps making the funniest remarks all during dinner. Our hostess gets up and makes a toast. Then Bill proposes a toast, and in his napkin is all the food he has spit out, and it goes all over the table. I think it was the funniest evening I had ever spent with Bill. He was ferocious.**

The show I loved doing was in Tokyo, in 1985, with Ungaro, Jean Muir, Issy Miyake, Hanae Mori, and Mariucci Mandelli of Krizia. I'll never forget it. We each were assigned a huge room backstage for our models and clothes. And here is Jean in this vast room with only one little rack. All jersey dresses, all black, navy, or brown. She might have had a couple of hats, but nothing else. I felt so sorry for her. I thought: Bless her heart, she's going to flop. We had hats, we had jewelry. She brought her own girls, English ones that nobody knew. And the first time we rehearsed, she had a guy at a piano singing this tough, honky-tonk music. Well, it was as if I had never seen a fashion show before. It was the most terrific thing I'd ever seen. We all looked so passé, so old hat, and so pretentious. Even Issy, one of the most innovative designers, somehow looked out of it. It was just unbelievable. I was crazy about Jean.

But the road show to end all road shows was the one we—Halston, Oscar, Stephen Burrows, Anne Klein, and myself—did in November 1973 at Versailles. Bill Cunningham, the street-and-society photographer at the *Times*, recently said that the Versailles show was "the Valhalla of American fashion—and everything was all downhill after that." Versailles *was* a triumph for American fashion, though I don't see how anyone would ever know. There was no press coverage, except in the *Times* and *Women's Wear*. If there was a film, it's been lost. And there were only a handful of Americans in the audience, including C.Z., who was one of the organizers.

In retrospect, I can see how Versailles became almost an untouchable subject. It is true that, in the beginning, we had everything going for us. We had Liza Minnelli, fresh from winning an Oscar for *Cabaret*, singing "Bonjour Paris" as all fifty of the American models, dressed in beige, came out on a stage piled with luggage. We had Liza's godmother, the singer and actress Kay Thompson (*Funny Face*), doing the choreography. We had Joe Eula designing sets. And though we didn't realize its significance at the time, we had black models, like Billie Blair and Pat Cleveland. We didn't hire them thinking they would look modern next to the haughty French mannequins, though that would be their impact, and the beginning, too, of the black models' reign in Paris. We hired them because they were the models we could afford.

Seeing all this more clearly now, I suppose even the idea (which was Eleanor Lambert's) of putting five of us up against five of the French—Ungaro, Pierre Cardin, Marc Bohen of Dior, Givenchy, and Saint Laurent—was so naïvely attractive that one could almost forget the French didn't give a shit about American clothes. After all, no American designer had been accepted in Paris since Mainbocher dressed Wallis Simpson and Lady Mendl—and that was before the war. Only in the areas of art, literature, and entertainment—through Hemingway, Rauschenberg, or the sheer banana brilliance of Josephine Baker— had Americans seduced the French.

But no matter what we had going for us or against us, it didn't compare to what we did to ourselves. The bitchery and paranoia among the American designers, especially displayed by Halston and Anne Klein, nearly turned the whole thing into a disaster. Sure, we ended up eclipsing the French on their turf. Sure, the French socialites threw their programs at us in ovation. But it could have so easily gone the other way. And not because the French were any better, but, rather, because we were so terrible to one another. I remember saying glumly to Fallon, as we

*At Versailles, talking with
Kay Thompson.*

sat in our box watching the French segment—they had gone first—"I don't believe
that I've spent all this time and money to come to Paris and have the French bury
us." That's how *defeated* I felt by what was transpiring behind the scenes.

Although the French probably had a few hysterical moments themselves,
they obviously saw what an opportunity they had. Marie-Helene de Rothschild
was taking care of social matters. She would exhaust the silver department of her
own house, as well as those of her friends, for the grandest of the dinners, at Versailles after the show. As props for the ten outfits that each designer was allowed
to show, there would be a pumpkin coach for Dior, a rocket ship for Cardin, a
gypsy cart for Ungaro. They also had a forty-piece orchestra, Rudolf Nureyev, the
nude dancers from the Crazy Horse, and Miss Baker herself. Seventy years old
and wearing a rhinestone body-stocking, she was going to come out singing "It's
Impossible" and dragging a big fur coat.

On the other hand, we had a backdrop that, when it was hung up in the
Versailles theater, fell two feet short of the stage floor—a picture of American
provincialism that I don't think even Grant Wood could have rendered. "It looks
like the laundry" is how Eula described his shrunken drapes, which through a

mistranslation, had been measured in yards rather than meters. He went out and bought a roll of white seamless paper, and, using black stove polish and a broom, sketched the Eiffel Tower. That was our set.

By noon of the day of rehearsals, the battle for turf had begun, with Halston informing everyone that Liza would only appear in his segment.* Livid, Oscar got on the phone to Raquel Welch, who was making a movie in Spain, and implored her to be in *his* segment. I don't know what was worse for Liza to contemplate—her friend Halston's unsporting manner or the thought of being upstaged by a sex bomb—but she soon settled the matter. She would perform as planned, and Raquel stayed in Spain. Meanwhile, Halston had begun to work on Anne, now sobbing and smoking like a chimney. Donna Karan, who was Anne's assistant at the time, recalled in a conversation for this book: "She knew the others were totally against her. It was horrible. But you know, they didn't feel that she belonged there. She was *sportswear*." Anne was also Eleanor's client; and a less potent choice, we thought, than the original one, Jimmy Galanos, or the second, Geoffrey Beene, both of whom had turned Eleanor down (citing, I believe, the hazards of working with other designers). Fed up with the viciousness, Kay Thompson walked out.†

I was having problems of my own. I had planned to do a kind of Noël Coward number to Cole Porter music, and had brought over a couple of male models to give it the right glamour. In fact, I was the only designer using men. But with everybody walking out or crying over one thing or another, the day was shot by the time we got to rehearse, and after twenty-five minutes, someone from the French side came up and said, "That's it. Your rehearsal is over."

JOE EULA: **Bill, out of all of them, I can tell you, was Prince Charming. Oscar was out of sorts. Halston, who was at the top of his fame, ran the roost, and tried to intimidate everybody. It was just disastrous.**

*You can't say Halston had a dim appreciation of his star power. Among his models were Elsa Peretti, Marisa Berenson, Baby Jane Holzer, and China Machado.

†Fortunately she did not go far. Without Kay, in my opinion, to direct the opening number, we would have certainly perished in flames of amateurishness. And don't forget stars of Liza's stature weren't permitted by their recording labels to actually sing for these kinds of events. "Bonjour Paris" was lip-synched.

Decorum demanded the colossal illusion of civility for the party that night, at Maxim's. And here, Oscar held an advantage, having made many friends in Paris through his wife Françoise's connections. But as Halston's backer, Norton Simon, was picking up the $20,000 dinner tab, Halston seemed to feel the entire event, including the show, hinged on his presence. He made this horribly clear as we were heading back to Paris after rehearsals to dress for dinner. He announced he was pulling out of the show. Actually, what he said was: "Mr. Halston is leaving, and when Mr. Halston leaves, everyone will go with him." He had started referring to himself in the imperial third. Dreading another scene, and now embarrassed for him,* I got him into my car, where, oblivious, he continued to exult in a blue streak of "Mr. Halston . . ." Finally, in one of the few times in my life when I've broken my rule not to get involved in a fight, I turned to him and said, "Ah, will you shut up."

I thought I understood American clothes; above all, I thought I understood the lean, agile, racy glamour of American clothes. Yet no one was prepared for the shock, the next day, of seeing them on a bare foreign stage, with only a broomed sketch of the Eiffel Tower and on skinny black girls nobody had seen before. And, of course, that had been a fluke. But it was the honesty, the pure simplicity, of our presentation—which lasted only thirty-five minutes compared to the two hours for the French—that brought the audience to its feet and made Bohan later say: "After we saw the Americans, we looked like idiots." Well, we had *behaved* like idiots. So if Versailles was Valhalla—and I'm not sure it really was—then it was impossible to feel completely proud about it. But at least, in that moment, we were unified. I was backstage after the show when Saint Laurent and Givenchy came up, and Hubert said, "You people have tamed Paris. You showed us modern clothes."

The road shows, especially in America, would continue to be a big part of my business for the next twenty years, and I loved the funny things that would

---

*A good seven or eight years earlier, when he was Bergdorf's custom milliner and still relatively unknown, Halston and I used to have lunch from time to time, at La Caravelle, and he couldn't have been a nicer, or funnier, luncheon companion. He once described his first meeting with the ancient hatmaker Lilly Daché, whom he had gone to see about a job. She had him over to her apartment and as they were talking, Halston noticed that she kept spritzing the air with a perfume atomizer she had by her side. He couldn't understand why this was necessary, then he realized that, with every squeeze of the atomizer ball, she was silently passing wind.

The Versailles show.

happen, and of course the women I got to know. But while still in the middle of that crazy decade, I received one of the harshest talking-downs of my career. It came from Eugenia Sheppard. One day she said, "You know, I'm so sick of hearing that you're going on the road all the time. It's showing in your clothes." I was stunned. She went on, "Believe me, you should go back to making clothes for New

From left: Michael Vollbracht, Adolfo, and Mary McFadden.

York gals, and not for those ladies in Iowa and Michigan. It's going to destroy you." She was absolutely right. I was paying too much attention to designing clothes for the lifestyles of those other places—and New York, and the status life of New York, will always be the inspiration for women in this country.

But then, Eugenia never missed a trick. She was the first journalist to write about me, because she sensed the social angle—and Eugenia could see how that story, the merger of society and fashion, was shaping up as one of the biggest stories of the sixties.

She was loyal as all get out, Eugenia. Loyal to those she liked. She once inscribed a book to me: "The only Bill I wouldn't mind paying."

9

"Luigi, What Do I Have?"

I bought Suzy Parker's apartment when she married the beautiful Pitou De Le Salle. That was at 444 East 57th Street, and I lived there, eventually knocking through to the next penthouse, until I bought my present apartment at One Sutton Place. For a while I had a place in Maine, at Christmas Cove—but it was nothing more than a fisherman's shack. And then one day in 1976, Billy Baldwin and I were

out looking at houses for sale in Connecticut, something we did a lot together, and I saw this wonderful old stone house. It had such dignity about it—and hideous red flocked wallpaper in the living room. The place was built in 1770 as a tavern on the old Albany Post Road. George Washington didn't sleep here, but apparently he had a drink here. During the First World War, it had been used as a rest home for wounded soldiers. I thought that was very attractive. The house came with six acres, and I bought the adjacent apple orchard, or what was left of it. Twenty-one acres in all. I moved in a few months later.

There's no question that I find houses and decorating absolutely fascinating. That really turns me on. That's when I get excited. I'd love to have the chance to do one more house. In fact, a few years ago I had several conversations with Chessy and Jacquelin Robertson, the Jefferson authority, about building a house, maybe near the water. Then I got out of that idea. Too ambitious. You see, when you're approaching eighty, you stop to think: Do I really want to do this? You stop to think altogether when you're turning eighty.

Anyway, the Connecticut house suits me to the ground. Like 444 and One Sutton, it has gone through various transformations, some more subtle than others, but all connected to the reinvention process—with pauses and full stops and, inevitably, tabula rasa, a clean start. At the time I bought the Connecticut house I was seeing a lot of Slim and, of course, Billy; and the initial decoration shows their influence, especially Billy's, with its sense of tidiness and unostentatious luxury. I adored Billy. Little jockey of a guy. But, boy, could he eat. Like Niki, he knew every story—every Daisy Fellowes story, every Pauline de Rothschild story.* Between them they knew everybody who had flair. Billy knew everybody in America, and Niki knew everybody in France and England. Billy did all of Kitty Miller's homes, and Bunny Mellon's. He did Cole Porter's apartment at the Waldorf Tower. There was something else that made Billy's rooms special: Many were never photographed. The clients wouldn't allow it. So here were these beautiful rooms, a reflection of their owners' taste, personality, and wardrobe—all things that Billy carefully considered—and nowhere do they survive except in the memory of the people fortunate enough to have seen them.

*And like Billy, born in Baltimore. Pauline favored nearly empty rooms that emphasized a few good pieces. She had an enormous influence on Billy, as did Frances Elkins and Van Day Truex.

"LUIGI, WHAT DO I HAVE?"

Billy Baldwin on Nantucket,
where he had a cottage.

That in itself may demonstrate a virtue. In their orderliness and sense of discretion, to say nothing of their mysteriousness, Billy's rooms truly exemplified the ideal of the private life.

The living room of the Connecticut house has always been rather simple—it is, after all, a tavern converted into a country house. In its first phase, the chairs were covered in chintz, and on the now-white walls were Catesby and Audubon engravings, some of which I hung below the windows. There were many more objects on the tables—boxes, English stirrup cups, horsey things—and a collection of mocha ware jars and mugs in a Welsh dresser in the dining room. It was very traditional, American. I never did curtains. Well, for one thing, it's a man's house, so I don't see why you need them. And I just think windows should be wide open and big. I've always been a believer in bringing the outside in.

STEVEN KAUFMANN: **There was a time when the Connecticut house was very different, when he knew Slim. It was cozier, because she was a cozy lady. I think Bill loved her decorating taste, and his house was more comfortable then. I think it's**

very cold now. Two or three years ago he did have a lamp, between the white chairs in the living room, and if you squinted very hard, you could read. Of course, during the day you have the light from the windows, so you can see. But usually there's a dog sitting on the couch, and that's more important.

I absolutely believe in Pauline de Rothschild's theory that lamps are the most jarring note in almost any house. She only brought them out at night when they were needed. Otherwise, they were to be banished, like the Hoover sweeper.

LOUISE GRUNWALD: **When Bill and I were young, he was collecting plaid boxes. They were Scottish; you'd find them in the market in London. But my point is, Bill always had his own point of view. There's been a metamorphosis in his style—paring down, paring down, and an escalation in grandeur. Listen, the Sutton Place apartment is very grand. But it's interesting that he never made the Connecticut house grand. He had those Catesby prints and the chintz. But you would never have done a Rorschach test and said Mario Buatta.**

Eventually, in the late eighties, I removed all the prints, sending them to the warehouse, and put up eighteenth- and nineteenth-century architectural drawings, all of them larger in scale and grouped together at one end of the living room. The chintz was replaced with white cotton slipcovers—or mattress ticking on the sofa, which is German, as big as a boat, and from a Berlin house in the thirties.

Gone, too, were most of the small objects. I suddenly realized that I couldn't stand the idea of a house full of mementos and crapola . . .

Today, the house does have a much more spare look, with fewer pieces of furniture, and not long ago I had the original maple floors in the living room and front hall stripped and stained a light Swedish gray—another influence. But the clearing-out process, which began in the mid-eighties, when I redid 444, represented more than a rigorous new approach to decorating. I had gone through a very stuffy, disapproving period—the result of taking myself too seriously—and I could see that what I needed was not more artifice or camouflage, but rather, just the opposite. I needed more clarity. And looseness.

LOUISE GRUNWALD: **We went to Munich, to this great dealer. This was twenty years ago. He had beautiful things and he showed Bill this and that, and Bill said, "Oh, I have that." Finally the dealer said, "What else do you have?" And Bill turned to me and said, "Luigi, what do I have?" We were in the drawing department. Anyway, we ended up each buying a drawing by Couture. And I said to Bill, "That's a name you'll remember." I mean, that was Bill. But he was charming to admit it:** *Luigi, what do I have?* **And that's why we love him. There's a façade, but it's a tongue-in-cheek façade.**

When I first moved to Connecticut, friends often came to stay for weekends, and it's never exactly quiet, even now. There's usually someone for Saturday or Sunday lunch—Nina Griscom, Blaine. When Brooke Hayward and Peter

Maps in the Connecticut dining room.

Duchin moved up here, I loaned them my guest cottage for a few months while they were waiting for their house to be finished. I've known them forever, it seems. Brooke is one of the last eccentrics. She is someone who's led a very full and interesting life—and you see this in her house, which is as far from conventional as you can get. She's crazy about her two little birds. They go everywhere with her. She'll go into the stores up here with one little fellow perched on each shoulder. They sleep on the pillow next to her at night. How does Peter feel about that? I wouldn't know. *That* seems a rather personal question, don't you think? I've known Peter a bit longer, since the sixties, when he was married to his first wife, Cheray. Peter is the most adorable, old-shoe of a guy. He's one of those real men you just can't help liking. He's disheveled; up here, he's more than disheveled. Unshoveled. He's sincere and real and great fun. Loves to laugh and drink.

So they lived in my guest house for quite a while. Then on the day they were packing up, they suddenly said, "We've decided to stay. It's much better here. We'll just stay here forever." I wasn't sure they were kidding.

Christmas saw the usual gang—Stevie, Glenn, somebody from San Francisco, whoever was at loose ends. I put the tree up in the dining room. Brooke and Peter would often be here for Christmas Eve dinner. Then, for two memorable years, Jessye Norman came from her place in Westchester. We had met one evening at "21" and gotten along like a house afire. She'd come here with her miniature keyboard; we'd all sit in the living room and after she had found the right key, she would sing carols. In German, French, and Spanish. It was such a treat. She would sing "Silent Night" in German. Just beautiful.

BLAINE TRUMP: **I will never forget going to his house about three years ago for a summer lunch. I went with David Linley and Ruth Kennedy. And we had meat loaf and mashed potatoes, the pepper jelly, and then lemon meringue pie. I mean, we rolled out of there. That was a twenty-pound lunch. But that's Bill. He doesn't give a damn about it being precious or fussy—it just has to be great food. Simple and American, and wonderfully presented. He's all about presentation.**

For me, one of the most critical aspects of judging a room is whether it belongs to the person in it. There has to be a connection between the choices and the personality of the owner. I remember a time when you really and truly felt that it was uncool not to have modern paintings in your house. Now you go into someone's home and the owner thinks he's being so with-it by having a Lichtenstein or a Pollack on the wall; but, in the end, it doesn't look as if the owner belongs in that setting. You constantly see this disparity between people and the rooms they lived in.

Not long ago, when Annie Leibovitz was up at the apartment, doing a portrait, she said, "What is this phallic thing you have going here? Everywhere I look . . ."

"What do you mean?" I said, intrigued. We were standing in my bedroom, which has a large round Edwardian table in the center and, on it, many books and a five-foot-tall bronze of the Place Vendôme obelisk.

Pointing now to the obelisk and the two globes on either side, Annie said, "You don't think that's phallic, with the two balls?"

I just thought the three objects looked amusing together . . .

Someone whose taste has changed—and *not* changed—is John Richardson. I say that because John is continually collecting, continually adding to his surroundings, yet, in essence, he has had the *same* apartment wherever he has lived. Because he loves to have a lot of things around him, clutter. And, as I said before, if you talk to John you learn the most amazing things. His place in Connecticut—which is like a little pavilion at the back of his property, where he does his writing—is good example of what I mean by a connection. It's bursting with information—books, drawings, papers, quirky objects, rumpled cat-haired sofas, all crammed together in an atmosphere of English warmth and intelligence. It could only belong to John.

I had no such confidence when I started to collect. I know this because, plainly, there in a photograph taken of my bedroom at 444 for *Life* magazine (1963) is not only the fur-covered bed, the ocelot-patterned wall-to-wall, the leopard-skin rug, and the obvious eclecticism of an oriental wallpaper panel, but also, next to the bed, a throve of pottery owls. I was in no danger of displaying any unconscious symbolism. It was all too evident—exactly what you'd expect of someone eager to be perceived as a sophisticated extra man. And yet I *was* the extra man. And I was out every night. So, while perhaps straining to make a point, the style of 444 did convey something of the youthfulness and energy of the sixties. And up until then everything in fashion and decoration came from the old.

Mica and Chessy, of course, helped me with 444 and all its subsequent changes. No matter how much you think you know, it's essential to have a decorator, and, for a man, a bachelor, it helps to have a woman decorator. A woman thinks of things like the kitchen, the closets, where people will sit. She's practical. And Chessy had a great flair for mixture and color. She was much more daring about color than I ever would have been. Yet I didn't find her sensibility—or Mica's—so feminine, like, say, Nancy Lancaster's. It was their idea to do a smaller bath and larger dressing room at One Sutton. Which makes all the sense in the world. I mean, the idea of a bathroom with a fireplace and a tub in the middle and chairs—who the hell do you think you are, Crawford in *The Women*?

Several years ago I became friends with the California decorator Rose Tarlow. For reasons that must have to do with a sense of scale, the quest for glamour, or perhaps, simply, the water, America has produced an extraordinary number of decorators from California and the Midwest: Rose Tarlow, Michael Taylor, Mark Hampton, and, of course, Frances Elkins, whose brother was the Chicago architect David Adler and whose own style—the California look—was to run through Michael and now Rose. Michael was an adorable guy. Great fun to be with. He loved the rusticity of California, as well as what Mark once called "the Gold Rush sparkle" of glamour, and he combined both in his decorating, mixing natural elements like stonework with fine French pieces. Rose has a wonderful eye for choosing something offbeat. If she gets to London one minute ahead of me, and hits the shops, I'm lost. We always go for the same thing: big, quirky, oversized.

Was there anyone who personified the flying coattails of New York more than Mark Hampton? That old Hoosier was gregarious, articulate—well-educated and self-educated. Go to a museum with Mark and he would absorb everything there was to be absorbed. His rooms were always rooms of affluence and security. He would be the first to say they weren't the most original. But they were remarkable for taking on the owner's personality. He and his wife, Duane, were a compelling force in the life of New York, as a couple, and I think his legend was built as much on her as on him. She did much to secure his sense of self.

> MICA ERTEGUN: **The apartment at 444 became more and more sparse. And then he started going to London more, and buying things. I remember two rugs which I liked very much. He changed his paintings quite often. The apartment was always leaking, because it was a penthouse. And he had a butler who was some number. Bill's life was much more social then.**

Going to London is like a pilgrimage. Well, I like to crawl back to familiar places. I'd get to the Connaught, have dinner at Harry's Bar with Marguerite Littman, and catch up. Spend hours talking and eating and drinking. The next day I'd head straight for Carlton Hobbs. There's no one who can top him. Whether it's for something Russian, French, or English, Carlton has the eye. Afterward, I'll drop by Ciminino on Pimlico Road. Or maybe Westenholz. Just behind Pimlico, at the end of an alley, is the small shop that belongs to Christopher Gibbs. He's one of the most handsome men in London and, of course, he's had an antiques shop for years. Knows everybody. John Richardson introduced us, and it was Christopher who sold me the huge Biltius painting of the muskets and standards that helped push the style of 444 in a new direction.

Another dealer I like a lot is Axel Vervoordt in Antwerp. I first heard about him from Susan Gutfreund, but I don't think anyone could have prepared John and me for what we saw: a castle—Kasteel van's Gravenwezel—set in the Flemish countryside and filled with objects and furniture that were very old, yet because of their scale and simplicity looked so modern. And I adore Axel's wife, May. Can't understand a word of what the other is saying, but somehow we communicate. It's an incredible place to go. Beautiful land. Enchanted way to go shopping.

By the time I bought One Sutton, I had the confidence—and, quite honestly, the means—to do the kind of apartment I wanted, and I think it says more clearly who I am than the Connecticut house does. It had once belonged to W. R. Grace, and in it's original state, before the apartment was split in two, the din-

The living room and bedroom at One Sutton.

ing and drawing rooms were next to each other. Apart from replacing the windows and floors, I made no structural changes. My bedroom (formerly W. R.'s dining room) is very much of a piece with the living room, as it was in the last redesign of 444. Both rooms are square—the easiest kind to decorate—and there's a feeling of openness, brought out by the high ceilings, the bare windows, and the drama going on outside, the bridges and river traffic.

Although the only things I brought from 444 are the silver tree trunk and the Biltius painting, there have been one or two constants in my collecting. I am invariably drawn to World War I things, and have two Jagger bronzes of soldiers. Also, I love animal things. One of the more unusual things I found (at Carlton Hobbs) was a pair of Russian bear sconces. Made of bronze, they're about two feet high and hang on either side of the Biltius painting in my bedroom.

Everything has been kept spare—more spare than any other place I've lived. Yet, for me, there's a great sense of serenity. I spend most of my time in the bedroom, reading or on the phone, and when friends drop by, we usually sit there.

My bedroom at 444, captured by Life *magazine.*

Over the years, with John's guidance, I've developed a passion for sculpture. Last summer, I remember, I was dying to buy something. Well, I'd been cooped up for so long. (And I've always believed you should buy something when you shouldn't. It gives you such a lift, and you'll find a way to pay for it somehow.) So I called a dealer friend of mine in Geneva. We chatted awhile. Then he described a ten-foot head he had. Maybe it was only a seven-foot head, but even that seems rather large, don't you think?

Anyway, I'm nuts about the statue I did end up buying. It's the remains of a bronze breastplate from a second-century B.C. equestrian statue. Greek. It had been under water for centuries, decaying. It's beautiful—it would look absolutely marvelous in a plain, plain room. In fact, not long ago, I replaced a pair of antique side tables in the living room with two new bronze tables that Mica had made. Again, it's about lightening. I also brought out from storage a large canvas in muted shades of orange and brown. Most people, when they see it, think it's a painting—a Rothko or something like that. But it's a fifteenth-century Peruvian funeral robe stretched on canvas. I think it's as modern as it could be. At one point, I had a lot of drawings in this room, but Stephen Sills suggested I take them down, and he was right.

I must say I know of no one who attempts to learn so much about rooms and furniture as Stephen. I don't find those other new people that interesting. They'll say, "Oh, I've been inspired by Syrie Maugham or Elsie de Wolfe." Well, of the two decorators in our time whom men shouldn't be inspired by, it's those two. Both were good decorators and revolutionary—Syrie Maugham with her all-white rooms and certainly Elsie de Wolfe made Edwardianism look so passé. But they weren't great decorators. Stephen did a list for a magazine in which he mentioned the Cuban-born decorator Emilio Terry, who designed the theater and so many of the objects at Château de Groussay. Anyway, Stephen and his partner, James Huniford, just finished doing Brooke de O'Campo's place in London, and I think they're pleased with it. They'll often go into a dealer's shop, see something, and say, "That's very Blass." And the dealer will say, "Should I send him a picture?" I've bought several things like that. They're right. It's funny: Another decorator had some pictures sent to me, but I didn't want any of it. It was all brown furniture and I don't want any more brown furniture.

Right now, I want painted stuff, or light stuff, or things made of steel. Something different. No, Stephen and Ford have everything I like. A marvelous eye.

MICA ERTEGUN: **In the beginning, when he bought One Sutton, he hired a chef and a staff to come once or twice a week, because he wanted to give dinner parties. And that lasted about two months, and that was it. And that's another apartment where you have no place to sit. And there's no coffee table. You sit in the big, big sofa, and you don't know what to do with your drink. And he doesn't care. He doesn't want you to be comfortable because he doesn't want you to stay too long.**

I've never had a drawing room or sitting room that was very comfortable. I did in the country when I had chintz and overstuffed furniture. I've never thought it wildly important for a guest to stay . . . *twenty minutes?*

STEPHEN SILLS: To me, One Sutton is very comfortable. It's a more dramatic stage set for Bill. He was so magnificent-looking in it—smoking the cigarette, in the suit with the loosened tie—when I first met him. It's designed to be a setting, a backdrop for him, and it works beautifully. That apartment has a great modern clarity. Bill was always a kind of modernist in decoration, even when he was collecting oriental things. At One Sutton, everything is old and antique, but the selection of objects is so streamlined. It's all about forms and volume, because everything is bigger-than-life scale. Again, it's like an opera set. So it doesn't have anything to do with decorating as most people know it. It's not about fabric or curtains. It's about objects. And they're all theatrical objects. Everything has such a bravado about it.

10

The Geography of Islands

In February 1981, I was invited to speak at Silliman College at Yale. Plainly, for someone whose contact with university life had been confined to a handful of cocktail-hour excursions to the Princeton Club with Ed Guild at the start of the war, this was a flattering endorsement of experience. I went up to New Haven with Tom and Gail and Slim Keith. Gail would later remember that afternoon at Yale as the single best day of the more than twenty years she worked for me— better than the glamorous galas or all the fancy trips abroad. I spoke to the men at their college. We had tea. They eagerly bombarded me with questions about fashion and my early years in New York. Then they took us to dinner at Mory's. Halfway through dinner, the Whiffenpoofs came out to serenade us. Well, there wasn't a dry eye in the place. It was the best and the brightest. Young men in their prime, and they're singing.* For me, what made the day especially right was that Slim got such a kick out of it. She, too, felt included.

Slim had entered my life a decade before, although we saw each other occasionally in London, in the sixties, during her marriage to her third husband, Sir Kenneth Keith, a British merchant banker, who, I suppose, had the misfortune of following Howard Hawks and Leland Hayward, to say nothing of the

---

*Later I had the Whiffenpoofs come to New York, for a Blassport show in the Pool Room at the Four Seasons.

men who had pursued her—leading off with Gable and Hemingway. Sir Kenneth probably saw Slim as the catch of all times, while she, weighing everything on life's scales, figured she could do worse than to marry a man who owned a large estate in Norfolk and spoke regularly to the prime minister. Socially, she did much to enhance her husband—not, in the opinion of some, the most likable of men—but after ten years with Sir Kenneth, Slim bolted, and returned to New York. We became reacquainted through Irene Selznick and Claudette Colbert, friends of Slim's since her marriage to Hawks, and Claudette often had her down to stay in Barbados, though the exquisitely temperate Claudette admitted that her old friend could sometimes agitate her.

Certainly Slim did nothing in small measures. And those who, in a sense, signed on with her were treated to the full, upending blast of her personality—

Slim during her marriage to Leland Hayward.

the stimulating, slightly bitchy conversation, the conscientious way she made
guests in her home feel at ease (indeed, her wide knowledge of housekeeping),
her fleecing humor, and the thoughtfulness of her gifts. You were never in any
danger of having a dull time with Slim. She brought a great deal to life—just
pure old-fashioned life. I remember one Christmas Slim asking if she couldn't
take Gail's young son, then about six, to the *Nutcracker*. Jerry Robbins had once
told her you should take a child to the *Nutcracker*—to see it with him and
through his eyes. Well, the kid was delighted, and dazzled by her.

So Slim and I began seeing a lot of each other. At first it was weekends at
her country house in Connecticut. A colony of New Yorkers, many from the fashion and magazine worlds, had begun to establish itself around Kent and Litchfield,
beginning with the Libermans, then the De la Rentas, followed by Diane von
Furstenberg, Abe and Casey Ribicoff, and John Richardson, whose place was just
down the road from Slim's. The weekends generally passed in a pleasant blur of
book-reading, house-hunting (for me), gossip, and eating, followed by the usual
fervent promises to go on a diet. When Slim was on one of her extended jaunts to
Barbabos, or to Martha's Vineyard to visit Lillian Hellman, her letters were filled
with warmth and perceptive wit. She had this to say about Hellman, on Feb-

ruary 22, 1977: "She is as bracing and salty as ever. Snapping at little things and dealing quietly with big ones. She really lives a great part of her life in Braille. I think she sees very little. The makeup goes on cock-eyed, the food misses the plate, the clothes are dusty and soiled. She sees with her ears. But that brain is flashing away and gnawing at whatever swims by."

Rereading her letters more than twenty years later, I am struck, too, by how essentially autonomous Slim was. Obviously this played a significant part in her appeal to men: no ball and chain, here. On the other hand, she seemed to recognize no true north in her internal compass. There was direction but it was without a sense of destination, and though she frequently spoke of wanting to belong to someone, it was mostly from old habit rather than real need. For I don't think Slim felt that she could belong to anyone.

I could say the same of myself. But did she understand the geographical properties of islands?

Like only a few glamorous women I have known whose humor could be piercingly accurate, Slim was not afraid to take the blow if a joke suddenly turned on her. Once, on a trip to Egypt, after furiously conceiving a plan to buy fabric from the bazaar and hiring a local seamstress to make her some djellabahs (muumuus would be closer to the truth), she invited me to her room so she could model the first results.

"Oh, my God," I said, wincing, "Ma Kettle."

The woman who had been the inspiration for Bacall's cool character in *To Have and Have Not* threw her head back in laughter. That was the end of Slim's dressmaking scheme.

There were limits, however, to her tough give-and-take. After buying some swans for her place in Connecticut, she considered giving the house a suitably swanlike name.

"I guess I can't call it 'Swan Lake,'" she observed.

"How about 'Swan Song'?" I said.

Slimbo, as I sometimes called her, was not amused.

When I found my own house, in 1976, I let her invade my life further, accepting her suggestions for making the place comfortable and cozy, two words I have almost bleached from my vocabulary. But let's give credit where credit is

With Claudette and Slim at a party.

due: Slim expertly gave comfort—in her food, manners, and confidences. She had not been christened Big Mama by Truman for nothing. And at sixty, even with a few more pounds around the middle, she was still beautiful. She was still Slim. So one did not feel invaded. Besides, for me, I knew that full occupation was not possible.

CASEY RIBICOFF: **Slim, in my opinion, was wonderful in his life for a time. She had great taste, and maybe at times he had better taste. But together it was exciting for them to go shopping and wandering. I remember they came to Washington, in 1978, when Russell and Carolyn Long were giving a farewell party for Abe and me. They were cozy and giggly. They came up to the Senate. It was fun. But it sort of alarmed me that she was so bossy with him. She would say, "No, we will not take the nine o'clock shuttle, we'll take the nine-thirty." I remember her tone and I thought, Oh, lady, that's not going to work.**

*Jerry Robbins
on Helen de
Rochas's boat
in Greece.*

By then, Slim had had her falling out with Truman over the publication of "La Cote Basque."* The problem with Truman, of course, was that he had ingratiated himself with Babe and Gloria and Slim, and all those fashionable women. It was the sort of ingratiation where he would stay with them and come and sit on their beds at night and talk to them. They would tell him all their secrets. And he was so sympatico, it never occurred to them that he could be dangerous. And Slim was particularly close to him. After the article came out, he didn't exist for her. For Babe, too. It was as if they had been publicly exposed. I didn't think the story was all that damaging, but it would be if it was written by someone you trusted. It brings to mind Elsa Maxwell, who made her living throwing parties at other peoples' homes and then telling them: "Oh, by the way, you're in my book." People would panic: "Oh, my God, what do you think she's going to say?" So they would give her a check for a couple of thousand dollars or buy her a new dress. "Put me in the book, yes; but put me in kindly." It was the same with Capote: He lied about many things, but he never lied about his in-

*In *Esquire*, 1975.

tention to write a book, and I think his women friends were afraid that what he would come out with would be much worse than it actually was.

Slim was devoted to Jerry Robbins. They had been lovers the summer Leland left her for Pamela Harriman, and she stayed friendly with him. The fact that Jerry swung both ways would not have been a serious obstacle for a woman as sophisticated and self-determining as Slim. Nevertheless, seeing Jerry with one of his boyfriends brought out a possessive streak in Slim that displayed itself with surprising cruelty. In 1976, Jerry had fallen in love with an aspiring photographer named Jesse Gerstein, then nineteen years old. They had met at Bloomingdale's, a detail that Slim seized on, adding, in Jerry's presence: "Yeah, in the basement." I liked Jesse. So did many others who knew him. He was a sweet, attractive kid. Jerry brought him to my house in Connecticut a couple of times for dinner—or rather Slim brought them, and then she wouldn't speak to Jesse.

This possessiveness was continually breaking through her affections. It might have bothered me if it hadn't been outweighed by her stronger qualties, and if I had thought there was any chance I could be possessed. Shortly after I started seeing a lot of Slim, I had a call from Swifty Lazar, inviting me to lunch. Swifty and Mary Lazar were very much a part of Slim's life, and they had become friends of mine. I met him at the King Cole Bar at the St. Regis.

"I'm going to tell you something," he said. "You seem like a nice chap. But I can't let you get caught in the Slim trap. She's out for Slim. She doesn't have an ounce of loyalty. And I don't want you to get taken in by her."

Sound advice for any man, but I'm afraid, in this case, he truly had the wrong man. "It's not likely, Irving," I said. "I just have a good time with Slim."

That was the uncomplicated truth. Slim and I had great times together. She had a marvelous mind, alert to the smallest details (though I realize now that it was the larger points that eluded Slim . . . such as understanding another person). Our weekends soon had lapsed into very enjoyable weeks abroad: Spain, Greece, where we shared Helen de Rochas's boat with Oscar and Françoise and visited the Erteguns in Turkey. Not my idea of heaven—the boat part—but I stuck it out for a week before leaving to spend a few solitary days in London. Slim knew I couldn't be easily confined, and, I believed, she had enough intimations to realize that I was perfectly happy to be alone. Yet we huge laughing fits. Although

the archaeological details of our Nile trip, which we made with the Fairchilds, now escape me—owing perhaps to the four of us being driven at a death rate through the desert by an Egyptian movie star—I do recall our last night in Cairo. Slim and I had fallen into a conversation with an Arab gentleman in the hotel bar. He was dressed in the most beautiful robes, the whole regalia. Handsome beyond anything. As I had caught the flu, I didn't linger. But I could see that Slim was completely charmed by the man. Her last words to me as I headed for bed were: "He's going to arrange for us to go through customs tomorrow."

So the next morning we got down to the lobby, and there was this man waiting in a bordeaux red polyester leisure suit with white stitching. I said, "You've got to be kidding." It was the same man. He was just a common petty official. We didn't vocalize our surprise at finding him so utterly transformed, but instead stifled it until our jaws ached.

On the plane back to New York, Slim composed the following letter, which she gave to me later:

> *Welcome home my dear friend,*
>
> > *Even though you are sitting beside me at the moment*
> > *that I write this and I could turn to you right now and tell you*
> > *how very rare and special you are . . . as always the words and*
> > *feelings are still-born on my lips but not in my heart. I know*

you know that and that you recognize and feel the warmth and
love that fills that empty room which stands between us. It isn't
an entirely empty room at all. It is filled with understanding,
appreciation and luxurious affection. It is just that we are never
in that room at the same moment . . .

Ma Kettle.

In the summer of 1981—our last together, as it would turn out—Slim and I decided to rent a house on Nantucket, along the bluff in 'Sconset. She would stay in the main house, I would take the small guest cottage; we would bring our dogs, and we would rest, read, and go on the long-promised diet. That was the plan. I said, "Okay, let's do it. But no nonsense. I just want to get thin. So, don't let's have exquisite little meals. Let's follow a diet." It was not entirely unknown to me, in the weeks before we left for Nantucket, that Slim had other expectations for that summer; friends had issued warnings of a rumor of a premeditated marriage strike. Swifty's words in the King Cole Bar now came swiftly back to me. But it wouldn't be until much later, until well into the fall, that I realized how extensively this apparent certainty had traveled on the grapevine. And by then, embarrassed, I had clammed up.

C.Z. GUEST: **I mean, she had a goddamn nerve to expect him to marry her. I never really liked Slim. She was so bitchy. She'd come up to me and say, "Oh, little Lucy, are you still writing your column?" And I'd say, "Yeah, why don't you get one." She thought she was an intellectual. And then this thing with Blass. I was so appalled. How dare she! They had been friends for, what? Twenty years? Somebody told me, "Oh, Slim is going to marry Bill Blass." I said, "You've got to be kidding?" It broke up their friendship. She really didn't care for his feelings, did she?**

I don't recall now how many nights I stayed on Nantucket, but after the first candlelight dinner, with Slim dressed up (and me in my usual summer slob attire), I could see that our plan of quiet evenings, low-fat meals, and reading and playing with the dogs wasn't the only one in operation. Unbeknownst to me, Slim had arranged a monthlong schedule of dinner parties and houseguests, the first of whom had already descended. There is no way that I can fault Slim for the way she ran things; she did it beautifully. Only I am not a person who can be run. And, of course, as soon as this thought takes hold, my immediate reaction is: I've got to get out of here. I flew back to New York after the first week, and spent the rest of the summer dodging the perplexed looks.

JOHN RICHARDSON: **I think Slim seriously felt that the love of a good woman could win him away. I mean, they were perfectly matched. They had both put on a bit of weight. They both knew the same people. They both had the same sense of humor. I think a lot of women in their time felt the same thing toward Bill. Not a hope. I mean, not a hope. I think that's one of the reasons why Bill used to keep people at a certain distance, because he didn't want this sort of thing happening. Slim simply wouldn't take the hint.**

Slim should have known how I felt about the subject of marriage, or even living with another person. We had spent enough time together by that point. I realized, naturally, that my hasty departure from Nantucket and the abrupt end of our friendship, combined with Slim's understandable feelings of bitterness, lent a certain undue mystery to the situation. People were curious. *What went wrong? What happened?*

In fact, that was the most curious part of all. It was rather Henry Jamesian—a mysterious situation in that nothing did really happen.

11

Fade Out to Black

I've always adored salmon croquettes. Where have all the croquettes gone?

Rolled in bread crumbs, with a little milk, and the freshest salmon, they used to be a staple of New York restaurants, along with other familiar dishes like tomato aspic and chicken à la king. After the war Bob Tompkins and I would sometimes meet for lunch at the old Midston House Hotel, on Madison, at 38th Street, where they had a restaurant called the Whaler Bar. The layout of the Whaler was overwhelmingly nautical, with portholes in the walls, and at brief intervals, a plate of clams or a dozen glistening oysters would pass before our gaze, conveyed by hidden pulleys. I'm sure I glimpsed a croquette or two.

Then they disappeared. You couldn't get croquettes anywhere in New York, for years. They weren't considered chic food.

The man who changed all that was Glenn Bernbaum, when he opened Mortimer's in 1976. Considering the role that Mortimer's would play in the social life of the eighties, and, with literary skewer, in Dominick Dunne's novel of the era, *People Like Us*, I suppose the decade began at that incautious moment. Already in his mid-fifties and living handsomely in a town house on East 52nd Street, bought with money he made in the men's shirt business, Glenn consulted no one when he decided to open his restaurant and move into the upstairs apartment. He just did it. And from the start, the place was jammed. Everybody came.

Brooke, Chessy, Mica, Nancy, Pat, Louise, Zip, Casey and Abe, the Boardmans, the Mortimers, Liz Smith, Aileen Mehle, all the gossip columnists. I think Nan had one meal a day there. And why not? The food was fabulous, like what you'd have in someone's home. Hamburgers. Chicken hash. Corn pudding. Strawberry shortcake made with buttermilk biscuits. And, of course, fresh salmon croquettes. The social success of Mortimer's used to drive Sirio at Le Cirque, and all the other restaurateurs, crazy. La Grenouille was the only restaurant Glenn liked in New York, and I'd take him there sometimes. But, you see, he realized that the last thing rich society wanted was another chic restaurant. It wanted a place of its own, a saloon that operated along the lines of a private club, where the unwelcome would be banished to Siberia, and the regulars would be given the better tables up front and the chance to feel triumphant that they were paying so little to enjoy such good food. As Glenn said often enough, with the gleam of a showman: "There's nothing the rich love more than a bargain."

Although Glenn himself was a product of a rich Jewish family from Philadelphia, it wasn't until he became a saloon keeper that he attained any real happiness—and even then he couldn't have derived all that much joy from shepherding ladies to their tables and generally playing the martinet. At the end of the day he still went up to his room above the store. I was fortunate at least to have had some sense of confidence doled out at my birth, and Glenn, despite a youth spent on Rittenhouse Square and his great snobbishness, had none of that confidence. He had appalling table manners and very low self-esteem—clear signs that beneath his intimidating surface was a desperately unhappy man. He couldn't hide it. I think in many ways he and Tiffeau had a deficiency in common. There was a tenderness in both of them that they didn't show to many people, but which I saw; yet there was something in their background, their nature, that caused them to have so little sense of self-value. It would be putting it mildly to say that Glenn didn't show a great deal of democracy in his choice of whom he wanted in his restaurant. He discouraged any gentleman from having a table of men, lest the restaurant became known as a gay hangout. It was an extreme form of self-denial that none of us could fathom. Yet it was Glenn who, in his own quiet, confused, belligerent way, established the first society event to raise money for AIDS research, Fete de Famille.*

*And, eventually, left his not-inconsiderable estate to the cause as well.

"Barnaby and Bill"
R. Tompkins
October 2

In 1986, Judy Peabody asked me if I might write some letters to people in the fashion industry requesting money for the Laboratory for AIDS Viral Research at New York Hospital. When no one replied, I went back to Judy. "Let's talk to Glenn," I said.

JUDY PEABODY: **I said, "Glenn? Cantankerous, adorable Glenn?"**
We took him to lunch and Bill told him and Glenn said, "Well,
let's have a street party." And that's how Fete de Famille started.
Glenn took charge and we got a lot of people involved because it
was Bill Blass and Glenn Bernbaum and Mortimer's. People
who didn't give two hoots about AIDS got involved. Hundreds of
people came. If Bill hadn't thought of going to Glenn, and if
Glenn hadn't suggested the party, the AIDS Care Center would
have never gotten started.

So Glenn was a man of conscience after all, despite his own inner quarrels. Some $7 million was raised by those Fete de Famille parties. Then, one day, at the

*With Lillian
Hellman and
Judy Peabody.*

peak of Mortimer's popularity, I got a phone call from the bartender, asking me to come and see him. Glenn was away in Europe and not due back until the following afternoon. The story the man laid out for me was too incredible—nobody would have believed it. Apparently Glenn's erstwhile friend, a Greek fellow who was the restaurant's manager, was planning to murder Glenn the next day. I thought the man was joking. So I laughed and said, "What time tomorrow?" I mean, Glenn wasn't exactly in line for a merit badge from his employees. Some hated him. But *murder*? Alas, the story was all too true. The friend had taken it into his head that he was going to inherit Glenn's money, and he wanted to hurry things along. Having boasted of his plan, however, he was easily caught and deported back to Greece. But the betrayal—and his own nearly fatal misjudgment—affected Glenn a lot, needless to say, and after that he didn't trust anyone. He always seemed to me to be someone who didn't fit in anywhere. Which certainly puts a different light on that raucous society epitaph "a place of its own." Yes. But where in the world did Glenn belong?

When the *Times* published Glenn's obituary, in September 1998, it noted somewhat cryptically that the cause of death was unknown, and then sped on to describe him as "a Solomon of bistro seating." The truth, as always, was more complicated than that. Glenn was in shocking shape physically. Hadn't been to a dentist or a doctor in forty years. When he decided to die, he just went up to his apartment and stayed there until his heart shut down. I think he helped himself along. He had drifted away from his family, and that's the way he would leave us. Fade out to black. I miss him more than I can say.

Sue Blair: **The first day I worked for Bill, he said, "Get Fairchild on the phone for me." So I called and said, "Hi, John." And he said, "Sue, don't call me John on the phone." Since we were friends, it never occurred to me to say Mr. Fairchild. Anyway, Bill then asked me to call Zipkin. I did indeed call him, but in the private phone book there were two numbers. The first one was busy, so I dialed the second. Boy, did I get yelled at by Mr. Zipkin. *"This is the private line for Nancy Reagan!"***

*Zipkin and
Mrs. Buckley
arriving at one
of my parties.*

Certainly Zip's ambitions, being social, meant that he gravitated toward
the superficial world of parties and gossip; and for an unattractive man, whose
father was a slumlord in the Bronx, he had risen way beyond his expectations. He
lived in one of his family's buildings—not in the Bronx, of course—but at 1175
Park. When I first met him, after the war, through Stevie, Zip was already han-
dling the family business. He would have lunch every day at Michael's Pub, which
was fashionable in the way that Mortimer's would be later. Zip was quick and
ambitious. He became very good friends with Ruth Tankoos and Ruby Schinasi—
stayed up all night playing cards with them—and for a while Diana. Betsy Bloomingdale was his best friend in Los Angeles, and he was her best friend. That's how
Zip became Nancy Reagan's closest confidant—through Betsy.

It was hard not to like Zip, if you got to know him. There was much about
him that was not likable, but then there was so much about him that was endear-
ing. He was famous for grabbing an extra party favor or goodie bag, offering as
an excuse for his habitual weakness, "It's for Mother," even after Mother, a nice

old girl named Annette, was dead and gone. I'll tell you who couldn't stand him was Eugenia. They were at a party once on the Revsons' boat when Eugenia suddenly started screaming at him. She was hysterical. "I can't take it! You shut up, you shut up! I can't stand you another minute. I'm getting off this boat!" She went ballistic over Zipkin always cutting people up with his opinions. I'm afraid he could be awful, though he could be accurate.

But, while Zip's critical tear-downs were often denuding, you were in no danger of him being indiscreet. He never told stories out of school. In fact, one of the pluses of a friendship with Zip was that he didn't talk about you once you were his friend. He would go to parties and people would sit around and say, "Did you hear about so-and-so?" And Zip would know the inside story, having heard it directly from so-and-so. He knew the facts. But he would never reveal them. Never say one word. So Nancy trusted him, and she was right to.

When Nancy and the president came to Washington, in 1981, she needed a New York confidant. Of course, she had her California friends, she had her Hollywood friends. I remember she became friendly on the telephone with Marlene Dietrich, whom she had not known in her actress days. Nancy would tell me of her late-night phone calls from Marlene in Paris, when she was reclusive. One night, out of the blue, Marlene just phoned the White House and asked to speak to Nancy. Well, why not? Marlene felt she was as big a star as life itself. And she was lonely.

I first met Nancy in California at a dinner at Edie and Bill Goetz's, when Ron was governor, and we talked briefly that night. She was instantly the most charming, offhand, unpretentious woman. She showed enormous interest in people. We saw more of each other after she moved to Washington, and I started making clothes for her. She was dressed primarily by Adolfo for daytime, and by Jimmy Galanos for important dinners. Adolfo* represented the highest scale of expensive clothes in our country for years, after Norell's death. Beautifully made. And Nancy appreciated that. At the first inauguration, she wore something from Jimmy for the ball, and for the gala the night before, which Frank

---

*Adolfo, a.k.a. Fito, closed his business five years before I sold mine. Unaccountably, people are surprised to find we are such good friends—maybe because designers so rarely are. But I've known Fito almost since the day he arrived in New York from Havana in 1951. He's such a marvelous man. He has books sent to me from London all the time, odd and unusual books about that period between the wars, which I'm so infatuated with. He's decent and nice. He looks like a little bird, yet he's not at all a person one should underestimate.

That's my bald head as Nancy and the president
make a suprise entrance at the Phillips.

Sinatra organized, she wore a black velvet dress of mine. Which *Women's Wear* said was a knock-off of Saint Laurent's. Which indeed it was.

As First Lady, Nancy had a gift for establishing intimacy with someone, which was not only spontaneous and natural, but was also jarringly different from her cooler public image. Shortly after the inaugural, I went down to Washington to do a benefit show at the Phillips Collection. Jennifer and Laughlin Phillips, along with Oatsie Charles, asked me if I thought the Reagans would come. I said I doubted it. "But let's ask them." The fact that they did come caused such a sensation, because it was the first time the Washington press corps had seen them at a social occasion other than a state dinner or a White House function. They didn't stay—they were going on to a private dinner somewhere—but everyone was tickled. Nancy came in with such enthusiasm.

Warmth is the most attractive quality in a woman, I think. It goes way beyond manners and, coming from a beautiful woman, it is almost enslaving. Slim had it. So did Pamela Harriman. And though she belongs to the nineties, so did Princess Diana. Marguerite Littman took me to lunch with Diana a month or so before the sale of her dresses at Christie's in New York, in 1997—that fateful, flower-banked summer. Marguerite had thought I might be helpful to her, and Diana had said, "Oh, I'd love for him to come to lunch." The minute we walked into Kensington Palace she was there to greet us. It was just the three of us. Midway through lunch, which was at a small table in the drawing room, Diana put her hand on my arm and said, unexpectedly, "What sign are you?" I'm only mildly interested in astrology, but, given where I was—and the hand resting on my arm—I decided to go along with it.

"Cancer," I said.

She smiled, victorious. "I knew it, I knew it," she said. "Because I am, too."

Later, when Diana came to New York for the auction, I gave a lunch for her at the apartment. She wanted Henry and Nancy Kissinger, and she wanted Jessye Norman. We were only eight. Daniel Boulud came and did the food: cold pea soup, sea bass in a potato crust, warm individual chocolate cakes with pistachio ice cream. Afterward I brought him out. Diana got up from the table and went to greet him. How gracious, I thought.

Nancy Reagan at the Waldorf
for an awards ceremony.

*With Missy Bancroft
at my sixtieth birthday.*

Nancy would come to New York from time to time. I remember one night at the Buckleys, just the four of us for dinner. For some reason or other the president couldn't come. Anyway, it was a sweltering summer night, and the Buckleys didn't have air-conditioning. To make matters worse, their King Charles spaniels, so relieved to see their mother and father after an absence, started relieving themselves all over the place. Not puddles: stacks. One here, one over there. We kept spotting stacks everywhere. At one point, when nobody was looking, I whispered, "Pat!"—and pointed to the ceiling. She thought there was one up there, too. We didn't know what we were going to do after dinner. Then Bill started playing the piano and I started singing, so you know how desperate we were to try to think of something to do.

But Nancy was marvelous on those kind of occasions. She was crazy about Bill Buckley. She simply gave a great deal to people she was fond of. Then she appointed me to the Arts and Humanities Commission, with Frank Sinatra and Betsy. I remember the *Times* called me and asked, "Why do you suppose you were chosen?" I said, "God only knows." Nancy rang me when the story appeared and said, "You should never answer like that. You should have said,

John Richardson.

'Because I'm going to be terrific at it.' " And I said, "Well, Nancy, frankly, I was very startled. If you had given me a little warning . . ."

It was wonderful going down to the White House. I would take Laura Montalban, my assistant, and Yoshimi Yamashita, my fitter. Nancy would have the three of us for lunch; if it was summertime we'd be out on the portico. I remember being there once on my birthday. Nancy, too, was a Cancer, and she knew my birthday, but she made no mention of it—until we were about to have dessert and out came a big cake in the shape of a Seventh Avenue shipping box. It had caramel icing and it said: BILL BLASS LTD, 550 SEVENTH AVENUE. It was such a sweet gesture. I don't know that Laura was impressed, since she had grown up in Hollywood, but Yoshimi was terribly impressed by the friendliness shown to her. That was so typical of Nancy. She put people at ease.

SUE BLAIR: **I must say Bill changed my life in the years that I worked for him. For one thing, he hired me. He used to get all these invitations, for opening nights and so forth. He didn't care,**

Tim Healy.

so I went. I had the best time in New York because of him. For the opening of the Costume Institute shows, he'd buy ten extra tickets for the after-party. Nobody in the office wanted to go. So I'd invite my friends and we'd go and have a great time. That was all because of Bill. He liked everybody to have a good time.

The eighties were certainly good years for business. People think the nineties were so good for fashion, but the real money was made in the eighties. We had clients who spent, easily, $200,000 a year on their clothes, which must be small change to a woman like Suzanne Saperstein, the blond Californian who apparently now outspends even Mouna Ayoub in haute couture. But the difference, then, was that designers had many, many clients—not just one trophy— willing to spend substantial sums on their clothes. It was a reflection of the booming economy, but also the expansive social life in this country. No one questioned what they were spending—and, in less visible ways, they still don't. The year after I sold my business* and turned the design over to Lars Nilsson, a very capable young man, a Swede trained in Paris, we had a suit in the line that cost $13,500. It was made of the most extraordinary fabric—a lacquered lace. They sold that suit in Palm Beach, sold it in Dallas. They sold a dozen. Nobody questions $13,500.

More critically, these were years in which you felt that making a name for yourself—indeed, *lasting*—was not only still the main objective in this notoriously shaky business, but that it was also still possible. And by then I had lasted forty years. The designers coming along at the time, whether Perry Ellis or Donna Karan or Carolyne Roehm or Michael Vollbracht, all felt, with good reason, that they were in it for the long haul. They had talent, but more, they had merchants like Philip Miller of Saks and Marvin Traub of Bloomingdale's willing to take a chance on them. And editors willing to give them pages of editorial without the equivalent in advertising—unthinkable in today's numbers-oriented climate. I doubt Marc Jacobs would have survived those early years without the inevitable duo of El and Hel—Ellin Saltzman and Helen O'Hagan of Saks—to see that he received orders and attention.

And although I was at a different place in my career, and seemingly content with my share (you'd think), I, too, received an unexpected boost—from Anna Wintour, when she took over American *Vogue*. I say unexpected because it's very difficult for a designer associated with one decade to get a foothold into the next with the magazines. Well, you're old hat. But Anna always made a point of including me. I'd never known an editor-in-chief to arrive so early in the morning to look at clothes; eight o'clock wasn't unusual. She'd come in, get a cup of coffee, and if the model had arrived—fine; we'd start. And then, one by one, young women dressed in black would crawl into my office looking like guilty schoolgirls. That's the way the junior editors of *Vogue* looked. Guilty as sin. Because their headmistress was already there.

Yet, funnily enough, I don't remember thinking that fashion in the eighties was excessive. To be sure, it was a time of poufs and panniers and brioche hair. But I think the excess—and the spirit of triumphalism—was more evident in peoples'

*To an employee of many years, Michael Groveman.

houses and decorating. Carolyne, then married to Henry Kravis, was doing their magnificent apartment. The Steinbergs were in play. You can point to other eras—the Regency, the twenties—that saw a similar dedication to form and achievement; except that in the eighties, thanks (I guess?) to the media, it was much less hidden. The opulence was there for everyone to behold and envy. Then it ended. Like that.

For me, the decade brought a significant reversal: I wanted less, not more—fewer objects and stuff around me, but also, with few exemptions, less contact with the people who had made up my world. This was easier to accomplish than it might seem. I simply went up to Connecticut on weekends and closed the door. I hadn't started to get old (I measure everything by age, if you can't tell), but I was beginning to feel exceptionally tired—tired of the duty-list of parties and obligations to be snappily met like a returning train, tired of the bullshit. I'd always been able to balance a love of fashion with the suspicion that it was counterfeit (a suspicion, at times, ignobly borne: *I'm in advertising*). And for as long as my career kept happening, I told myself this was okay. This was the routine. But I am someone who has lived for most of his life in search of one ideal or another. Ed. Niki. Billy. Someone who was a brother, a friend, a mentor—but, in any case, someone you could look up to. That's the part of fatherlessness that hardly anyone gets: It's not the loss of love you mind most; it's the loss of a permanent ideal. And even after you stop actively looking for that person, the feeling itself never goes away.

In the mid-eighties, Dick Solomon, who had briefly owned Saint Laurent, asked me to join the board of the New York Public Library. I was surprised and flattered. Reading had always been a passion. Annette was on the board; so was Brooke. Much later, I was asked by Marshall Rose—a wonderful, altogether sane fellow—if I would make a donation* to kick off the library's fund-raising drive. All this was supposedly for the good but, for me, the real goodness came in the form of Tim Healy, the former president of Georgetown University who, in 1988, had succeeded Vartan Gregorian as head of the library. I had never met anyone like Tim. Vastly intelligent, big and red-faced and jolly, he immediately singled me out as someone he wanted to know. We became very friendly. Tim was Irish

*The proposed sum, $10 million, was matched or exceeded by other members.

in wit and thirst only. "I belong to all Irish societies," he once said, "but I'm not Irish. I am probably the linear descendant of an eighteenth-century sheep thief."

At the time I wore braces and so did he; and I would find the most outrageous ones, prancing with naked girls, to give to him. And Tim would find things he thought I didn't have. He loved food, and we both loved smoking and drinking. It was a revelation to me to see a priest enjoy his martinis. But then Tim was not very priestlike—you wouldn't have thought it for a minute—and he didn't have to make an effort to show that his heart was in the right place. It just was. So for only the second time in my life I had found someone with whom I not only felt a great male bond, but could also say anything under the blessed sun.

ANNETTE DE LA RENTA: **I introduced John Richardson to Tim Healy. I took them fishing together, along with Bob Hughes, up to our place in Canada. It was amazing—I mean, you didn't want to miss breakfast because you hated to think what they were saying. It was just very, very funny. So John could understand the attraction that Bill would have for Tim. He was intelligent enough to understand Bill, and to understand that Bill would be much more interested in what he could do for the library. It was Tim who touched Bill, and Bill is very difficult to touch. I mean, if the Church stands for anything, it's compassion, and the Jesuits for intelligence. And compassion without soupiness. Soupy is everything that both Tim and Bill would hate. John is very much more sentimental. You can make John cry.**

Fairly soon after we met, Tim asked me if I would be chairman of the East Coast selection committee for the Rhodes Scholars. A first, I laughed. "For God's sake, Tim, I barely finished high school, how can I do something like that?" He assured me there would be academics to take up the slack. "I think it will be a good experience for you," he said. Well, I got such a kick out of those meetings, though none of my friends was the least bit impressed. We met for three days, interviewing young men and women, all ably Oxford. And I never agreed with one of the academics on his choices. I felt the finalists ought to have some charisma to handle themselves as Americans, not just as scholars; that they should have a personality that would make the experience more agreeable to them, and to the notion of being Americans. There was a Japanese girl who was so appealing, but she wasn't chosen. Though I suppose that's why Tim wanted me on the committee—for a different take.

Then one morning in late December 1993, Marshall called me in Connecticut to say that Tim had died the previous night. He had been returning from his Christmas holiday in Arizona when he collapsed at Newark airport. It was a heart attack. The rest of that day passed in an oblivion of phone calls and disbelief. Then, on the night before his funeral, which was at Saint Ignatius Loyola Church on Park Avenue, he was laid out, and I saw something I had never seen before. The audience for his wake was almost entirely male.

How exceedingly right, I thought. He was so beloved by a generation of young men. And no longer young, I was now among them.

JOHN RICHARDSON: **To my mind, meeting Tim Healy was one of the crucial things in Bill's life. First, he got involved in the library. He's always read an enormous amount. People had this idea, even in the old days, that there were handsome hustlers. Not at all. Bill was taking the dogs for a walk, reading, reading, and having the odd drink. Father Healy took an interest in Bill, and Bill was absolutely besotted. It was not a sexual thing. This was a father figure, somebody he could revere . . . I would think, for someone like Bill, who, outside his professional world, has no psychic or spiritual center, here was this man. He was bringing Bill out more and more. Because people used to imagine these glamorous young models throwing themselves at Bill, and that's not what he wanted at all. He wanted a strong, dependable daddy. And, in a funny way, Healy was the one who came along. It was one of the best things that ever happened to Bill.**

12

Bedazzled Boy

When I set out to write this book I didn't know where it would lead me. I knew, of course, that I would have to write about the Depression and the war as well as that narrow window of time when I first came to New York and all was clear to me, with the crystalness of youth, what I would become. I knew, too, that I would have to write about certain people, if only to make them *be*, again, in these pages.

For several weeks I've been undergoing what I can only guess is post-memoir syndrome. Should I have mentioned . . . ? Did I say enough about so-and-so? And all I can say is: I'm sorry, maybe next time. These freak-outs are usually accompanied by a last-minute sprint for immortality. How shall I be re-membered in the end? I could claim one or two firsts. And I am reminded that in the early seventies, before designers became pundits, William Safire wrote a column in the *New York Times* in which he assigned a few of us in fashion a coun-terpart in political life. I was Nelson Rockefeller: "establishment, secure, power-ful, the taste arbiter, a man you can go to the well with."

And, well, yes, there is that.

But I see now what this memoir has been from the beginning. All my ex-periences, all my yearnings, have been those of a typical American boy becom-ing a typical American man, except that my focus was on clothes rather than on oil drilling or banking or some other great commodity. It was a typical Ameri-can success story after all. The small-town background, the war, New York.

So this is how I think I will be remembered . . .

BILL BLASS MEAT LOAF

1 cup chopped celery

1 cup chopped onion

2 pounds ground sirloin

½ pound ground pork

*½ pound ground veal (ask your butcher
   to grind the meats fresh)*

½ cup minced parsley

1 ½ cups fresh bread crumbs

*1 egg beaten with 1 tablespoon
   Worcestershire sauce*

Salt and pepper

Pinch of thyme and marjoram

1 12-ounce bottle Heinz Chili Sauce

5 strips bacon

Preheat oven to 350 degrees.

Sauté celery and onion in butter. Combine with
the meats, parsley, bread crumbs, and egg with
Worcestershire sauce, add seasonings, and
form loaf. Top with chili sauce and then bacon.
Bake 1 hour. Remove from the oven and rest—
not you, silly, the meat loaf.

Serves six

A Note from the Editor

Bare Blass was conceived over a two-martini lunch at the Four Seasons in New York in September 1999, although a memoir had obviously been in Bill's mind for much longer. From the outset, we did not want a book that adhered to conventional time, but rather one that freely skipped back and forth over time, much as Bill's memories did. Our conversations began in the late fall of 2000 at his house in Connecticut and continued every weekend for the next ten months. He read chapter 1 on September 2, 2001, as he sat on the back patio catching sun, and I took a swim in the pool.

Remarkably, we never had a serious disagreement, and only one anecdote was deleted from the final text, on the grounds that it invaded the person's privacy. Bill was much less interested in having me set down the events of his life than in making sure I understood them. At one point, after seeing a draft of the war chapter, he said, "Kid, I don't know if you can understand what this period meant to me. It's really a man's story." Those invaluable words gave me a key to the shaping of his character.

I am—we are—indebted to the many friends who agreed to be interviewed for this book, and to the staff of the Bill Blass Archive, which has kept drawings and personal papers dating back to his childhood. Bill and I met for the last time on Friday, June 7, 2002, to discuss minor galley changes. He died the following Wednesday.

Cathy Horyn
June 16, 2002

INDEX

Blass, Bill *(cont.)*

automobile endorsements of, 39,
70

British accent of, 5, 56–57

cancer diagnosis and treatment
of, 11–15

childhood drawing by, *4*

childhood of, 3–5, 8, 9–10,
23–25, *24, 25,* 32

Connecticut home of, 9, 71, 99,
128, 129–33, *132,* 136, 139,
144–45, 164

corporate logo of, 6, 11

design sensibility of, 7, 8–9, 45,
47, 48–49, 58–59, 71–73,
93, 106, 127–28, 130–32,
134–40

dogs owned by, 9, 10, 99–100,
161

drawing ability of, 5–6

driving record of, 39

first fashion jobs of, 5–6, 10–11,
19–21, 47, 50, 54

fittings and, 85, 86, 93–94

food and, 4, 40–41, 116–17, 118,
121, 133, 151–52, 168

fragrances and, 77–79

ideal woman as described by, 83

licensing arrangements and, 70,
77–79

Maine home of, 128

masculine aesthetic of, 8–9,
36–37, 65–66, 71

meat loaf recipe of, 168

men's collections of, 44–45,
70–77, 79

money matters and, 26, 28, 30,
57, 107

New York apartments of, 8–9, 10,
48, 57, 58–59, 71, 128, 131,
134–35, 136–40, *137, 139*

nicknames of, 27*n*, 57

office of, *85,* 85–86

personality of, 3, 10, 22, 25–26,
27, 30, 47, 67–68, 164

photographs of, *2, 6, 7, 12–15, 18,
19, 22, 24, 25, 27, 29, 31, 34,
36, 37, 39, 42, 46, 48, 55, 59,
61–63, 69, 70, 74, 75, 84, 85,
87, 88, 92, 93, 98, 101–4, 109,
114–16, 120, 123, 137, 143, 145,
153, 157, 159, 161, 168–69*

politics and, 113

prizes and awards won by, 19,
21, 70, 75–76

rise to prominence of, 54–55,
68–79

road shows of, 113–27

sexual issues and, 5, 10, 32, 37,
44, 61, 67, 71, 117–19

wardrobe of, 26, 45–46, 107

Blass, Ethyl Keyser (mother), 3, 6, 10,
18, 18–19, *22,* 22–25, 32, 36,
43

Blass, Ralph Aldrich (father), 15, 18,
22–23, 24

suicide of, 3, 9, 23, 26

Blass, Virginia (Gina) (sister), 6,
21–22, *22,* 24, 36, 43

Blassport, 79, 111–12

Blondell, Joan, 54

Bloomingdale, Betsy, 155, 159

Bloomingdale's, 163

Blumenthal, A. C., 63

Blunt, Anthony, 26

Boccia, Ed, 35, 37

All illustrations and photographs are used courtesy of Bill Blass, Ltd. Archives unless noted below. Grateful acknowledgment is made to the following for permission to reproduce the images on the pages noted:

Pages vi–vii (contents page): © Richard Avedon.

Page 2: © Richard Avedon, courtesy of Bill Blass, Ltd. Archives.

Page 7: N. Vreeland, courtesy of Bill Blass, Ltd. Archives.

Page 12: John St. Clements, courtesy of Bill Blass, Ltd. Archives.

Pages 15, 88: Howell Conant/Life Magazine. © Time Inc., courtesy of Bill Blass, Ltd. Archives.

Pages 29, 62: Mort Kaye Studios, Inc., courtesy of Bill Blass, Ltd. Archives.

Page 31: Denis Sheahan/WWD Archives, courtesy of Bill Blass, Ltd. Archives.

Pages 34, 36, 39, 42: Courtesy of Robert Tompkins.

Page 37: National Archives.

Page 46: Sheldon Ramsdell, courtesy of Bill Blass, Ltd. Archives.

Page 53: Courtesy of Steven Kaufmann.

Pages 61, 137: © Time, Inc., courtesy of Bill Blass, Ltd. Archives.

Page 69: Jack Robinson, © Vogue, Condé Nast Publications, Inc.

Pages 85, 157: Barbara Walz, courtesy of Bill Blass, Ltd. Archives.

Page 87: Women's Wear Daily, courtesy of Bill Blass, Ltd. Archives.

Pages 90, 142: AP/Wide World Photos.

Page 91: Courtesy of Bill Blass.

Page 92: New York Times, courtesy of Bill Blass, Ltd. Archives.

Page 93 © 1990 Ron Galella/Ron Galella, Ltd.

Page 97: Courtesy of Women's Wear Daily and Casey Ribicoff.

Page 98: Betty Furness, courtesy of Bill Blass, Ltd. Archives.

Page 101: Roger Prigent, courtesy of Bill Blass, Ltd. Archives.

Page 102: Howell Conant/Life Magazine © Time Inc.

Page 103: © Ron Galella, Ltd., courtesy of Bill Blass, Ltd. Archives.

Page 104: Otto Stupakoff, courtesy of Bill Blass, Ltd. Archives.

Page 114: Agência Fotográfica Vasclo, courtesy of Bill Blass, Ltd. Archives.

Page 115: Courtesy of Bill Blass, Ltd. Archives and Women's Wear Daily.

Page 139: Fred R. Conrad.

Page 145: Guy Delot/Women's Wear Daily.

Page 148: Courtesy of Helen O'Hagan and the Estate of Claudette Colbert.

Page 153: Bill Cunningham, courtesy of Bill Blass, Ltd. Archives.

Pages 155, 159, 160: Tom Iannacune/Women's Wear Daily.

Page 157: John McDonnell, The Washington Post.

Page 158: Garvin/Ron Galella, Ltd. © 1985.

Page 161: Jeannette Montgomery Barron, courtesy of Bill Blass, Ltd. Archives.

Page 162: Don Hamerman, courtesy of the New York Public Library.

Color Plates:

Color plate 1: Painting of Bill Blass and Niki de Gunzburg by Joe Eula, courtesy of Bill Blass.

Color plate 2: Courtesy of Bill Blass Ltd. Archive.

Color plate 3: Bill Blass's war notebook, photograph by Fred R. Conrad.

Color plate 4: *Clockwise from top left:* Marietta Tree, courtesy Bill Blass Ltd. Archives; Kit Gill, photograph © Saul Leiter, courtesy Howard Greenberg Gallery NY; Lauren Hutton, courtesy of Bill Blass, Ltd. Archives; Bill Blass photograph, Howell Conant/Life Magazine, © Time Inc.

Color plate 5: Advertisement by Jane Trahey, courtesy of Bill Blass, Ltd. Archives.

Color plate 6: Photograph by Mary Hilliard, © Vogue, Condé Nast Publications, Inc.

Color plate 7: *Clockwise from top: Vogue* cover courtesy of Bill Blass, Ltd. Archives; dress from Spring 1995 collection, courtesy of Bill Blass, Ltd. Archives; Britt Eklund, photographed by Francesco Scavullo.

Color plate 8: *Clockwise from top left:* Brooke Astor: Adam Scull/Globe Photos, Inc., © 1991; Nancy Reagan: Jon Simon/Ron Galella Ltd., © 1984; Nancy Kissinger: Adam Scull/Globe Photos, Inc., © 1991; Lynn Wyatt: Anthony Savignano/Ron Galella, Ltd., © 1987; Bill Blass after a show: courtesy Bill Blass, Ltd. Archives.

Color plate 9: The current New York apartment, all photographs by Fred R. Conrad.

Color plate 10: Painting by Robert Tompkins, courtesy of Bill Blass.